The Epic Tales of India:

15 Stories of Love, War, and Devotion from Hindu Mythology and Indian Literature

- ACHINTYA

"Stories have power. They delight, enchant, touch, teach, recall, inspire, motivate, challenge. They help us understand. They imprint a picture on our minds. Consequently, stories often pack more punch than sermons."

- Achintya.

FOREWORD:

India is a land of rich and diverse cultures, traditions, and religions. It is also a land of stories, stories that have been passed down from generation to generation, stories that reflect the values, beliefs, and aspirations of the people, stories that inspire, entertain, and enlighten.

Hindu mythology and Indian literature are two of the most prominent sources of these stories. Hindu mythology is the collection of narratives and teachings that form the basis of Hinduism, one of the oldest and most influential religions in the world. Indian literature is the body of works produced by the writers and poets of India, spanning across languages, genres, and periods.

The Epic Tales of India: 15 Stories of Love, War, and Devotion from Hindu Mythology and Indian Literature is a tribute to these two sources of stories. It is a collection of 15 stories that have been selected from various texts and traditions, such as the Vedas, the Ramayana, the Mahabharata, the Puranas, the Panchatantra, the Jataka Tales, and more. These stories are not mere retellings, but rather fictionalised adaptations that aim to capture the essence and spirit of the original sources.

The stories in this collection cover a wide range of themes and topics, such as creation, cosmology, morality, ethics, romance, heroism, sacrifice, justice, wisdom, and faith. They feature some of the most iconic characters and events from Hindu mythology and Indian literature, such as Brahma, Vishnu, Shiva, Ganesha, Rama, Sita, Krishna, Arjuna, Draupadi, Shakuntala, Vikramaditya, Kalidasa, and more. They also showcase the diversity and richness of India's culture and history.

I personally suggest kids to read these stories to improve their morals and values, these silly mythological stories (which most people claim them to be) are actually packets that contain tons of knowledge and ethics one should forever follow.

The Epic Tales of India: 15 Stories of Love, War, and Devotion from Hindu Mythology and Indian Literature is a book for anyone who loves stories. It is a book for anyone who wants to learn more about India's heritage and legacy. It is a book for anyone who wants to experience the magic and wonder of Hindu mythology and Indian literature.

How Ravana Lost Everything: A Story of Arrogance, Dominance and Desire

Ravana was the king of Lanka, a powerful island fortress that he had conquered from his half-brother Kubera, the god of wealth. Ravana was a mighty warrior, a master of magic, and a devotee of the god Shiva. He had ten heads and twenty arms, each holding a different weapon. He was feared and respected by all beings in the three worlds: heaven, earth, and the underworld.

Ravana had many wives, but his favourite was Mandodari, the daughter of the king of the asuras, the enemies of the gods. Mandodari was beautiful, wise, and virtuous. She loved Ravana and tried to advise him to be righteous and compassionate. But Ravana was blinded by his pride and ambition. He wanted to be the supreme ruler of the universe, and he challenged the authority of the gods.

Ravana was a complex and contradictory character. He was a brilliant scholar, a devout worshipper, and a generous ruler. He had mastered the four Vedas, the ancient scriptures of Hinduism, and had acquired many boons from the gods through his penance and devotion. He had built a magnificent city of gold and silver, where he provided for the welfare and happiness of his subjects. He had a large family of brothers, sisters, sons, and daughters, whom he loved dearly.

But Ravana also had a dark side. He was arrogant, greedy, and lustful. He was obsessed with power and glory, and he wanted to conquer all the worlds. He had a violent temper and a cruel streak. He did not hesitate to kill or torture anyone who opposed him or offended him. He had offended many gods and sages by his actions and words. He had stolen Kubera's flying chariot, Pushpaka Vimana, and his island kingdom of Lanka. He had also tried to lift Mount Kailash, the abode of Shiva, and had been crushed under it for a thousand years until he begged for mercy.

Ravana's appearance reflected his personality. He had ten heads and twenty arms, each holding a different weapon. His heads represented his knowledge of the ten directions, the ten senses, and the ten aspects of creation. His arms represented his strength and skill in warfare. His weapons included swords, spears, bows, arrows, maces, axes, shields, and more. He wore a golden crown and earrings, a red robe and cloak, and a garland of skulls around his neck. His eyes were red with anger and passion, his teeth were sharp and white, and his voice was loud and thunderous.

6

Ravana's behaviour was influenced by his ego and desire. He believed that he was invincible and superior to everyone else. He did not respect anyone's free will or dignity. He thought that he could take whatever he wanted by force or deception. He did not listen to anyone's advice or criticism. He ignored the warnings of his wife Mandodari, his brother Vibhishana, and his grandfather Malyavantha, who tried to persuade him to return Sita to Rama and avoid war. He also ignored the curses of various sages and gods who predicted his downfall.

One of the most important parts of the story is when Ravana abducted Sita from her forest hut. This was the turning point that led to his doom. Ravana had seen Sita in a dream and had fallen in love with her. He had asked his sister Shurpanakha to find out more about her. Shurpanakha had gone to the forest where Rama, Sita, and Lakshmana were living in exile. She had tried to seduce Rama, but he had rejected her politely. She had then attacked Sita out of jealousy, but Lakshmana had cut off her nose and ears with his sword.

Ravana was intrigued by Shurpanakha's description of Sita and Rama. He wanted to see Sita for himself and make her his wife. He thought that Rama was just a mortal prince who could not match his power and glory. He decided to abduct Sita by using a cunning plan. He asked his spy Maricha to help him in his scheme.

Maricha was a demon who could change his shape at will. He was Ravana's uncle and had been his loyal servant for a long time. But he was also wise and cautious. He knew that Rama was no ordinary man, but an incarnation of Vishnu, the supreme god. He had seen Rama's strength and skill when he had fought with him in the past. He had barely escaped with his life after being hit by Rama's arrow. He warned Ravana that kidnapping Sita would be a foolish and fatal mistake. He said that Rama would surely come after him and destroy him and his entire kingdom.

But Ravana did not listen to Maricha's advice. He threatened to kill him if he did not obey his orders. He told him to transform himself into a golden deer and run past Sita's hut in the forest. He said that Sita would be charmed by the deer and ask Rama to catch it for her. He said that he would then follow Rama into the forest and wait for an opportunity to snatch Sita away.

Maricha reluctantly agreed to do as Ravana said. He changed himself into a beautiful golden deer with silver spots and ruby eyes. He ran past Sita's hut and caught her attention. Sita saw the deer and was amazed by its beauty. She asked Rama to catch it for her as a gift. She said that she had never seen such a wonderful creature before.

Rama smiled at Sita's request and agreed to catch the deer for her. He told Lakshmana to stay with Sita and protect her while he went after the deer. He took his bow and arrows and followed the deer into the forest.

Maricha led Rama far away from his hut and then turned back into his original form. He fought with Rama and was wounded by his arrows. Before dying, he cried out in Rama's voice, "Help me, Lakshmana!" He hoped that Lakshmana would hear the cry and leave Sita alone, so that Ravana could take her away.

Sita heard the cry and thought that Rama was in danger. She urged Lakshmana to go and help him. Lakshmana hesitated, but Sita accused him of being selfish and unfaithful to his brother. She said that he did not care about Rama's life or her happiness. She said that he had a secret desire for her and that was why he did not want to leave her side.

Lakshmana was shocked and hurt by Sita's words. He tried to explain that it was a trick by the demons and that Rama was safe and strong. He said that he had sworn to protect Sita at any cost and that he would never betray his brother or dishonour her. He said that he had drawn a magic circle around the hut and told her not to step out of it for any reason.

But Sita did not believe Lakshmana's words. She insisted that he go and save Rama from danger. She said that she would rather die than live without Rama or with Lakshmana.

Lakshmana reluctantly agreed to go, but he warned Sita not to cross the circle or trust anyone who came near her hut. He said that he would return soon with Rama and prove his innocence.

As soon as Lakshmana left, Ravana arrived in his flying chariot. He disguised himself as a holy man and asked Sita for some water.

Sita was kind and generous, but she remembered Lakshmana's warning and refused to cross the circle. She said that she would give water to the holy man, but he had to come inside the circle to receive it. Ravana then revealed his true identity and told Sita that he had come to take her away as his wife. He praised her beauty and promised her riches and glory if she agreed to marry him. Sita was shocked and disgusted by Ravana's proposal. She rejected him firmly and said that she was loyal to Rama only.

Ravana was enraged by Sita's refusal. He decided to abduct her by force. He lifted her up in his arms and flew away in his chariot. Sita cried out for help and threw her jewels on the ground as a sign for Rama to follow her.

Rama and Lakshmana returned to their hut and found it empty. They saw the jewels on the ground and realised that Sita had been kidnapped by Ravana. They were filled with grief and anger. They vowed to rescue Sita and punish Ravana for his crime.

Rama and Lakshmana began their search for Sita with the help of Hanuman, the son of the wind god and the leader of the monkeys. Hanuman was a loyal friend and a brave warrior. He could fly across the sky, change his size, and perform many feats of strength and courage. He found out that Sita was held captive in Lanka, guarded by many demons. He crossed the ocean and reached Lanka. He searched for Sita in Ravana's palace and finally found her in a garden called Ashoka Vatika.

Sita was sitting under a tree, surrounded by demonesses who tormented her with harsh words and threats. She was pale and thin, but still radiant with grace and dignity. She had not given up hope of seeing Rama again. She had also not given in to Ravana's demands. She had resisted his advances and insults with courage and faith.

Hanuman approached Sita quietly and introduced himself as Rama's messenger. He showed her Rama's ring as a proof of his identity. He told her that Rama was alive and well, and that he was coming soon to rescue her. He also gave her a message of love and comfort from Rama.

Sita was overjoyed to see Hanuman and hear from Rama. She thanked Hanuman for his service and asked him to convey her message to Rama. She said that she was waiting for him eagerly, but also warned him of Ravana's strength and cunning. She said that he should be careful and prepared for a fierce battle.

Hanuman assured Sita that Rama would defeat Ravana and free her from his clutches. He asked her if she wanted anything from Lanka as a souvenir. Sita said that she did not want anything from Lanka, except a flower from the tree under which she was sitting. She said that the tree had given her shade and comfort during her captivity, and that it was a symbol of her devotion to Rama.

Hanuman plucked a flower from the tree and gave it to Sita. He then asked for her permission to leave. Sita blessed him and wished him a safe journey.

Hanuman decided to create some havoc in Lanka before leaving. He wanted to test Ravana's power and alert him of Rama's arrival. He set fire to many buildings and gardens in the city, including Ravana's palace. He killed many demons who tried to stop him. He also made a loud noise and challenged Ravana to face him.

Ravana was furious when he heard about Hanuman's deeds. He sent his son Akshaya Kumara, a brave and skilled warrior, to capture Hanuman. Akshaya Kumara fought with Hanuman and wounded him with his arrows. But Hanuman was too strong and fast for him. He killed Akshaya Kumara with his mace and continued his rampage.

Ravana then sent his son Indrajit, who was the commander of his army and a master of magic. Indrajit used his illusions and weapons to trap Hanuman in a net of ropes. He brought Hanuman before Ravana and his court.

Ravana was enraged to see Hanuman, the monkey who had dared to enter his city and cause so much destruction. He asked him who he was and why he had done such things.

Hanuman replied that he was the servant of Rama, the lord of the universe, and the messenger of Sita, the goddess of fortune. He said that he had come to Lanka to find Sita, who had been kidnapped by Ravana against her will. He said that he had seen Sita in Ashoka Vatika, where she was suffering under Ravana's tyranny. He said that he had given her Rama's ring and message, and had taken a flower from her as a token of her love. He said that he had set fire to Lanka as a warning to Ravana, and as a sign of Rama's power and wrath.

Hanuman then advised Ravana to return Sita to Rama and beg for his forgiveness. He said that Rama was the supreme personality of Godhead, who had descended on earth to uphold righteousness and destroy evil.

He said that Rama was invincible and irresistible, and that no one could stand against him. He said that Rama was coming soon with a mighty army of monkeys and bears, led by Sugriva, the king of Kishkindha, and Jambavan, the king of the bears. He said that Ravana should surrender to Rama and save himself and his kingdom from destruction.

Ravana was astonished and amused by Hanuman's words. He thought that Hanuman was a foolish and ignorant monkey who did not know his own strength or weakness. He thought that Rama was just a human prince who had been banished from his kingdom by his father. He thought that Sita was his rightful wife who had chosen him over Rama. He thought that he was the lord of the three worlds, who had defeated many gods and demons in battle.

Ravana laughed at Hanuman's advice and mocked him for his audacity. He said that he would never return Sita to Rama or bow down to him. He said that he would rather die than give up his pride and glory. He said that he would crush Rama and his army like insects, and make Sita his queen.

Ravana then ordered his guards to kill Hanuman for his insolence. But Vibhishana, Ravana's younger brother, intervened and stopped them.

Vibhishana was a pious and righteous brother of Ravana. He did not approve of Ravana's actions and tried to persuade him to follow the path of dharma. He said that Hanuman was a guest and a messenger, and that killing him would be a grave sin. He said that Hanuman had spoken the truth and that Rama was indeed the supreme lord. He said that Ravana should listen to Hanuman's advice and return Sita to Rama, or else face his wrath.

Ravana was angry with Vibhishana for siding with the enemy. He accused him of being a traitor and a coward. He said that he did not need his advice or his loyalty. He said that he would spare Hanuman's life, but only to humiliate him. He said that he would set fire to his tail and make him run around the city as a spectacle.

Ravana's ministers agreed with his decision and praised him for his cleverness and courage. They brought some cloth and oil and wrapped Hanuman's tail with it. They then lit the cloth on fire and released Hanuman from the net.

Hanuman felt a sharp pain in his tail, but he did not lose his composure or his confidence. He realised that this was an opportunity to create more havoc in Lanka. He used his power to make his tail longer and thicker, and to make himself bigger and stronger. He broke free from his captors and jumped from one building to another, setting them on fire with his tail. He caused more damage and chaos than before, and terrified the demons with his roar.

Ravana was shocked and furious when he saw Hanuman's escape and destruction. He ordered his army to capture him again, but they failed miserably. Hanuman was too fast and powerful for them. He reached the ocean shore and dipped his tail in the water to extinguish the fire. He then saluted Rama in the direction of India and flew back to join him.

Hanuman met Rama and Lakshmana at the mountain of Mahendra, where they were waiting for him with Sugriva, Jambavan, and other monkey chiefs. He told them everything that had happened in Lanka, and showed them Sita's flower as proof of her well-being. He also described Ravana's palace, army, and allies, and gave them an estimate of his strength and weakness.

Rama was overjoyed to hear from Hanuman about Sita's safety and love. He thanked him for his service and praised him for his bravery and intelligence. He also thanked Vibhishana for his kindness and support. He said that he was ready to wage war against Ravana and rescue Sita from his clutches.

Rama then asked Sugriva to mobilise his army of monkeys and bears, who had gathered from all over the world to help him in his mission. He said that they had to cross the ocean to reach Lanka, which was a hundred yojanas (about 800 miles) away from India. He asked for suggestions on how to do so.

Sugriva suggested that they could build a bridge across the ocean with the help of Nala, a monkey engineer who had a boon from Vishwakarma, the divine architect. Nala agreed to take up the task and asked for volunteers to help him collect rocks, trees, and mountains from various places.

Rama approved of Sugriva's suggestion and ordered his army to start building the bridge across the ocean. He also prayed to the ocean god, Varuna, to grant him permission and support for his project. Varuna appeared before Rama and blessed him with his consent and cooperation. He said that he would make the waters calm and stable, and that he would protect the bridge from any harm.

The monkeys and bears worked hard and fast to collect and transport the materials for the bridge. They wrote Rama's name on every rock, tree, and mountain, and threw them into the ocean. The rocks floated on the water by the power of Rama's name, and formed a strong and steady bridge. Nala supervised the construction and arranged the materials in a proper order and shape. Within five days, the bridge was completed, spanning a hundred yojanas in length and ten yojanas in width.

Rama was pleased with the bridge and praised Nala and his helpers for their skill and dedication. He then led his army across the bridge to Lanka, where Ravana and his forces were waiting for them.

A fierce and long war ensued between Rama and Ravana, lasting for fourteen days. Many brave warriors fought on both sides, displaying their valour and prowess. Many heroic deeds were done, and many tragic deaths occurred.

Rama faced many challenges and difficulties in the war. He had to deal with Ravana's magic, deception, and treachery. He had to fight with Ravana's powerful allies, such as Kumbhakarna, Ravana's giant brother who could sleep for six months at a time; Mahiravana, Ravana's sorcerer brother who could change his form at will; and Indrajit, Ravana's son who could become invisible and use celestial weapons.

Rama also had to endure many sorrows and losses in the war. He had to see his friends and allies wounded or killed by the enemy. He had to see Sita suffering in captivity, as Ravana tried to persuade or threaten her to marry him. He had to see himself doubted and accused by some of his own followers, who questioned his divinity and authority.

But Rama also had many sources of strength and support in the war. He had his faithful brother Lakshmana by his side, who always stood by him and helped him in every situation. He had his loyal friend Hanuman, who performed many miraculous feats of service and devotion for him. He had his righteous brother Vibhishana, who defected from Ravana's side and joined him with his followers.

He had his divine weapons, such as the Brahmastra, which he had received from his guru Vishwamitra; the Gandiva bow, which he had received from the god Agni; and the Sudarshana Chakra, which he had received from Vishnu himself.

Rama also had his own virtues and qualities, such as courage, wisdom, compassion, patience, humility, honesty, justice, and faith.
He followed the rules of dharma and respected his enemies as well as his friends. He never gave up hope or faith in his mission and his destiny. He always remembered his love for Sita and his duty to rescue her.

Finally, on the fourteenth day of the war, Rama and Ravana faced each other in a decisive duel. They fought with all their might and skill, using their weapons, words, and wills. They matched each other in every aspect, and neither could gain an upper hand.

Ravana used his ten heads and twenty arms to attack Rama from different directions. He used his various weapons, such as the Shakti, the Pashupata, and the Nagastra, to inflict pain and damage on Rama. He also used his taunts and insults to provoke and mock Rama. He said that Rama was a weak and foolish man who had lost his kingdom, his wife, and his honour. He said that Sita was his property and that he would never give her back to him. He said that he was the lord of the universe and that he would destroy Rama and his army.

Rama used his single head and two arms to defend himself from Ravana's attacks. He used his divine weapons, such as the Brahmastra, the Gandiva, and the Sudarshana Chakra, to counter and neutralise Ravana's weapons. He also used his calm and composed words to reply and refute Ravana's taunts and insults. He said that Ravana was a wicked and ignorant demon who had committed many sins and crimes. He said that Sita was his wife and that he would always love her and protect her. He said that he was the servant of God and that he would uphold dharma and justice.

The battle lasted for a long time, and both Rama and Ravana were exhausted and wounded. But they did not give up or surrender. They continued to fight with determination and courage.

At last, Rama decided to end the battle with his most powerful weapon, the Brahmastra. He invoked the weapon with a mantra and aimed it at Ravana's chest. The weapon flew like a blazing arrow towards Ravana, piercing through his armour and heart. Ravana fell down from his chariot, dead.

Rama had won the war. He had killed Ravana and avenged his wrongs. He had fulfilled his promise and duty.

Rama then went to Ashoka Vatika, where Sita was waiting for him with joy and relief. He embraced her with love and gratitude. He freed her from her captivity and restored her honour.

Rama then crowned Vibhishana as the new king of Lanka, as a reward for his loyalty and righteousness. He also performed the funeral rites for Ravana and his sons, as a gesture of respect and compassion.

Rama then returned to India with Sita, Lakshmana, Hanuman, Sugriva, Jambavan, and other monkey chiefs.

He crossed the bridge again and reached the shore of India. He thanked Nala and his helpers for building the bridge and asked them to dismantle it. He then thanked Sugriva, Jambavan, and other monkey chiefs for their assistance and friendship. He gave them many gifts and blessings.

Rama then proceeded to Ayodhya, his capital city, where he was welcomed by his father Dasharatha, his mother Kaushalya, his brothers Bharata and Shatrughna, and his people. He was crowned as the king of Ayodhya, and Sita as the queen. He ruled his kingdom with wisdom and justice, and brought peace and prosperity to his land. He was loved and respected by all beings in the world.

This is the end of the story of how Ravana lost everything: a story of arrogance, dominance, and desire.

The moral of this story is that one should not be proud, greedy, or lustful, as these qualities lead to one's downfall. One should also not harm or oppress others, as this invites one's destruction. One should instead be humble, generous, and faithful, as these qualities lead to one's success. One should also respect and protect others, as this brings one's happiness.

As for what happened to Ravana after his death, there are different versions and opinions. Some say that he was liberated from his cycle of birth and death, as he had died at the hands of Rama, who was an incarnation of God. Some say that he was reborn as a human or a god, as he had performed many good deeds and worshipped Shiva in his previous lives. Some say that he was condemned to hell or a lower species, as he had committed many evil deeds and offended many gods and sages in his life.

Urvashi's Adventures: A Divine Beauty's Encounters with the Human World

Urvashi was the most beautiful of all the apsaras, the celestial nymphs who lived in the court of Indra, the king of the gods. She was an expert dancer and singer, and could enchant anyone with her charm and grace. She was also very curious and adventurous, and often wished to explore the world beyond heaven. She had heard many stories about the human world, where there were different kinds of people, animals, plants, and cultures. She wanted to see them for herself, and learn more about them.

One day, she got a chance to fulfil her wish. Indra had sent her along with some other apsaras to perform at a yagna, a sacred fire ritual, conducted by a group of sages on earth. The sages had invited Indra and other gods to bless their yagna, and Indra had accepted their invitation. He had also decided to send some of his apsaras as a gesture of goodwill and appreciation.

Urvashi was thrilled to go to earth for the first time. She dressed herself in a dazzling white saree, adorned with jewels and flowers. She wore a crown of lotus on her head, and a garland of jasmine around her neck. She looked like a goddess herself, and all the other apsaras admired her beauty.

They flew down to earth in a chariot drawn by swans, accompanied by some gandharvas, the celestial musicians. They reached the place where the yagna was being held, and saw a large fire burning in a pit surrounded by sages. The sages were chanting mantras and offering oblations to the fire. They looked very serious and solemn.

The apsaras descended from their chariot and greeted the sages with respect. The sages welcomed them with reverence and gratitude. They asked them to sit on a platform near the fire, where they could watch the yagna. The gandharvas also joined them, carrying their musical instruments.

The apsaras began to sing and dance for the pleasure of the gods and the sages. They sang hymns praising Indra and other gods, and danced gracefully in sync with the music. They also displayed their various skills and talents, such as playing different instruments, reciting poetry, telling stories, and performing magic tricks.

Urvashi was the star of the show. She sang with a melodious voice that filled the air with sweetness. She danced with such elegance and agility that she seemed to float in the air.

She played the veena, a stringed instrument, with such skill that she could make it sound like any other instrument. She recited verses from the Vedas, the ancient scriptures, with such clarity that she could explain their meaning to anyone. She told stories from Indian mythology with such flair that she could make them come alive in front of everyone's eyes. She performed magic tricks with such finesse that she could make anything appear or disappear at her will.

Everyone was mesmerised by Urvashi's performance. The gods who had come to attend the yagna were delighted by her devotion and talent. The sages who had organised the yagna were impressed by her knowledge and wisdom. The animals who had gathered around the yagna were fascinated by her charm and grace.

But Urvashi was not satisfied by just performing for others. She wanted to see more of the earth and its wonders. She wanted to interact with more people and learn more about their lives. She wanted to have some fun and adventure on her own.

So, she decided to sneak away from the yagna site when no one was looking. She told one of her friends, Menaka, another apsara, that she was going to fetch some water from a nearby river. Menaka agreed to cover for her while she was gone.

Urvashi quickly ran towards the river, leaving behind her crown, garland, jewels, and saree on a tree branch. She did not want to attract too much attention with her dazzling appearance. She wore a simple yellow dress that she had borrowed from Menaka's wardrobe.

She reached the river bank and saw a clear stream flowing gently through green fields and forests. She saw some fish swimming in the water, some birds flying in the sky, some flowers blooming on the shore, and some fruits hanging from the trees.

She felt a surge of joy in her heart as she saw these beautiful sights of nature. She decided to explore them further.

She dipped her feet in the water and felt its coolness on her skin. She splashed some water on her face and felt its freshness on her eyes. She drank some water from her palms and felt its sweetness on her tongue.

She then walked along the river bank and saw some cows grazing on the grass. She approached them gently and stroked their backs. They moped softly and licked her hands. She felt their warmth and friendliness on her fingers.

She then climbed up a tree and saw some monkeys swinging from the branches. She joined them playfully and swung with them. They chattered loudly and pulled her hair. She felt their mischief and fun in her head.

She then plucked a mango from the tree and saw its golden colour and juicy pulp. She bit into it and tasted its tangy flavour and soft texture. She felt its nourishment and delight in her mouth.

She then jumped down from the tree and saw some children playing on the ground. They were running, laughing, singing, and dancing. They were wearing colourful clothes and carrying toys and instruments.

She approached them curiously and smiled at them. They smiled back at her and invited her to join their game. She accepted their invitation and joined their game.

They played a game called kho-kho, where one team had to chase and catch the members of the other team by touching them. Urvashi was on the chasing team, and she ran after the other children with speed and agility. She caught many of them by touching their backs, shoulders, or heads.

The children were amazed by Urvashi's skill and stamina. They cheered for her and praised her. They also asked her many questions about herself, such as her name, where she came from, what she did, etc.

Urvashi answered their questions with honesty and simplicity. She told them that she was an apsara, a celestial nymph, who lived in heaven with Indra, the king of the gods. She told them that she was a dancer and singer, who performed for the gods and the sages. She told them that she had come to earth for the first time to see its beauty and diversity.

The children were astonished by Urvashi's story. They asked her more questions about heaven, gods, apsaras, sages, etc. Urvashi answered their questions with patience and enthusiasm. She told them more stories from Hindu mythology, such as how Indra became the king of the gods, how Vishnu took different avatars to save the world, how Shiva destroyed evil with his dance, how Ganesha got his elephant head, how Saraswati became the goddess of learning, etc.

The children were enchanted by Urvashi's stories. They listened to her with rapt attention and interest. They also learned many lessons from her stories, such as how to be brave, kind, wise, loyal, humble, etc.

19

Urvashi was happy to share her stories with the children. She felt a bond of friendship and love with them. She also learned many things from them, such as how to be playful, cheerful, curious, creative, etc.

They played and talked for a long time, until the sun began to set in the horizon. They realised that it was time to go back to their homes.

They said goodbye to each other with hugs and kisses. They thanked Urvashi for her company and stories. They invited her to come again and play with them.

Urvashi thanked them for their hospitality and friendship. She promised to come again and play with them.

She then ran back to the river bank, where she had left her celestial attire. She put on her crown, garland, jewels, and saree. She looked like a goddess again.

She then flew back to the yagna site in a flash of light. She reached there just in time before anyone noticed her absence.

She rejoined the other apsaras on the platform near the fire. They were still singing and dancing for the gods and the sages.

She resumed her performance with renewed energy and joy. She sang louder, danced faster, played better, recited clearer, told more stories, performed more magic tricks.

Everyone was more mesmerised by Urvashi's performance than before. The gods were more delighted by her devotion and talent than before. The sages were more impressed by her knowledge and wisdom than before. The animals were more fascinated by her charm and grace than before.

But Urvashi was not thinking about any of them. She was thinking about the children she had met on earth. She was thinking about their smiles, laughter, songs, dances.

As Urvashi resumed her performance, she noticed that among the audience, there was a young man who looked very familiar to her. He had bright eyes, fair skin, curly hair, and a handsome face. He was wearing a white robe and a golden crown. He was sitting on a throne, surrounded by guards and ministers. He was none other than Ayus, the eldest son of Pururavas and Urvashi.

Urvashi felt a surge of emotion in her heart as she saw her son. She remembered how she had given birth to him on earth, and how she had left him with his father when he was still a child. She wondered how he had grown up to be such a noble and powerful king. She also wondered if he recognized her as his mother.

She decided to test him by singing a song that she had composed for him when he was a baby. She sang it with such sweetness and tenderness that everyone was moved by it. The song was about the love between a mother and a son, and how they were separated by fate.

Ayus heard the song and felt a strange connection with the singer. He felt as if he had heard the song before, in his dreams or in his memories. He looked at Urvashi and saw her beauty and grace. He felt a strong attraction towards her, but also a sense of respect and reverence. He realised that she was not an ordinary woman, but an apsara, a celestial nymph.

He asked his ministers who she was, and they told him that she was Urvashi, the most famous of all apsaras. They also told him that she had come to earth with some other apsaras to perform at the yagna of the sages. They praised her for her devotion and talent.

Ayus felt more curious about Urvashi and wanted to talk to her. He asked his guards to bring her to him after the performance. The guards obeyed his order and approached Urvashi.

Urvashi saw the guards coming towards her and understood their intention. She felt nervous and excited at the same time. She wondered what Ayus wanted from her, and what she would say to him.

She followed the guards to Ayus's throne, where he greeted her with courtesy and admiration. He asked her to sit beside him, and offered her some fruits and flowers. He then asked her about herself, where she came from, what she did, etc.

Urvashi answered his questions with honesty and simplicity. She told him that she was an apsara, who lived in heaven with Indra, the king of the gods. She told him that she was a dancer and singer, who performed for the gods and the sages. She told him that she had come to earth for the first time to see its beauty and diversity.

Ayus listened to her with rapt attention and interest. He asked her more questions about heaven, gods, apsaras, sages, etc. Urvashi answered his questions with patience and enthusiasm. She told him more stories from Hindu mythology, such as how Indra became the king of the gods, how Vishnu took different avatars to save the world, how Shiva destroyed evil with his dance, how Ganesha got his elephant head, how Saraswati became the goddess of learning, etc.

Ayus was enchanted by Urvashi's stories. He learned many lessons from them, such as how to be brave, kind, wise, loyal, humble, etc. He also felt a deep affection for Urvashi and wanted to make her his wife.

He asked her to marry him and stay with him on earth. He promised to give her everything she wanted and make her happy.

Urvashi was surprised by Ayus's proposal and felt conflicted about it. She liked Ayus very much and appreciated his qualities. She also felt a maternal love for him and wanted to protect him from any harm.

But she also knew that he was her son, even though he did not know it. She knew that it was wrong to marry him or stay with him on earth. She knew that she belonged to heaven and had to return there soon.

She decided to tell him the truth about their relationship and hope that he would understand.

She said to him: "O Ayus, you are a great king and a noble man. You have honoured me with your proposal and your generosity. But I cannot accept your offer or stay with you on earth."

Ayus asked her why not, and what was stopping her from being with him.

Urvashi said: "O Ayus, you are my son, born from my womb on earth. Your father is Pururavas, the first of the lunar dynasty. I left you with him when you were still a child."

Ayus was shocked by Urvashi's revelation and could not believe it.

He said: "O Urvashi, how can this be true? How can you be my mother and I your son? How can you prove it to me?"

Urvashi said: "O Ayus, you can verify it from your father or from the sages who witnessed your birth. You can also see the resemblance between us in our features and our talents. You can also feel the bond between us in our hearts."

Ayus was still doubtful and confused. He asked Urvashi to show him a sign that would confirm her words.

Urvashi said: "O Ayus, I will show you a sign that will convince you of the truth. Look at the sky and see the moon. He is your grandfather, Chandra, the lord of the night. He is also the lord of the apsaras, and he loves me as his daughter. He will bless you as his grandson and grant you a boon."

As Urvashi said this, the moon appeared in the sky, shining brightly and smiling kindly. He spoke to Ayus and said: "O Ayus, Urvashi is telling you the truth. She is your mother and I am your grandfather. You are my descendant and I am proud of you. You have done well as a king and a warrior. You have also shown respect and love for Urvashi. I bless you with long life, prosperity, fame, and happiness. I also grant you a boon. Ask me anything you want."

Ayus was amazed by the moon's appearance and words. He bowed to him and thanked him for his blessings and boon.

He said: "O Chandra, I am grateful for your kindness and generosity. You have given me more than I deserve. I have only one wish in my heart. I wish to see my father, Pururavas, who is in heaven with Urvashi. I wish to meet him and embrace him as my son."

The moon said: "O Ayus, your wish is granted. You will see your father soon and be united with him in heaven. But before that, you have to complete your duties on earth. You have to rule your kingdom well and protect your people from enemies. You have to perform many sacrifices and charities for the welfare of all beings. You have to follow dharma and uphold justice. You have to be a good husband to your wife and a good father to your children. You have to be a good example for your successors and successors."

Ayus agreed to do all that the moon had asked him to do.

He then turned to Urvashi and said: "O Urvashi, I am sorry for my ignorance and folly. I did not know that you were my mother and I offended you with my proposal. Please forgive me for my mistake."

Urvashi said: "O Ayus, there is nothing to forgive. You did not know the truth and acted out of innocence and love. I am happy that you have found out the truth and accepted it with grace. I am proud of you as my son."

She then hugged him and kissed him on his forehead.

She said: "O Ayus, I love you as my son and I will always watch over you from heaven. I will also pray for your happiness and success on earth. But now, I have to leave you and return to heaven with the other apsaras. We have completed our performance at the yagna and we have to go back to Indra's court."

Ayus said: "O Urvashi, I love you too as my mother and I will always remember you in my heart. I will also follow your teachings and advice on earth. But please, do not leave me so soon. Stay with me for some more time and bless me with your presence."

Urvashi said: "O Ayus, I cannot stay with you for long on earth. It is against the rules of heaven and earth. But I will stay with you for one more night and bless you with my presence."

She then asked the moon to grant her permission to stay with Ayus for one more night.

The moon agreed to her request and said: "O Urvashi, you can stay with Ayus for one more night on earth. But after that, you have to return to heaven without fail."

Urvashi thanked the moon for his permission.

She then asked Ayus to take her to his palace, where they could spend some time together.

Ayus agreed to her request and took her to his palace.

Urvashi was amazed by Ayus's palace, kingdom, achievements, virtues, and family. She felt proud of him as her son and happy for him as a king. She also felt a bond of love and respect with his wife and children. She blessed them all with her good wishes and prayers.

She then spent some time with Ayus alone in his chamber, where they talked about their lives and experiences. She told him more about heaven and its wonders. He told her more about earth and its challenges. They shared their joys and sorrows, hopes and fears, dreams and aspirations. They also sang some songs and recited some poems that they had learned from each other.

They felt a deep connection and understanding with each other. They felt as if they had known each other for a long time, even though they had met for the first time.

They then slept peacefully in each other's arms, feeling safe and secure.

The next morning, Urvashi woke up before dawn and saw Ayus sleeping beside her. She kissed him gently on his cheek and whispered in his ear: "O Ayus, it is time for me to leave you and return to heaven. I have to go back to Indra's court and resume my duties as an apsara. I will miss you very much, but I will always be with you in spirit. I will also come back to see you whenever I can. Please do not be sad or angry with me. Please remember me with love and gratitude."

Ayus woke up and saw Urvashi looking at him with a smile and a tear. He hugged her tightly and said: "O Urvashi, I do not want you to leave me and return to heaven. I want you to stay with me on earth and be my mother. I will miss you very much, but I will also respect your decision. I will not be sad or angry with you. I will remember you with love and gratitude."

They then got up from the bed and got ready to depart.

Urvashi dressed herself in her celestial attire, which was dazzling white, adorned with jewels and flowers. She wore a crown of lotus on her head, and a garland of jasmine around her neck. She looked like a goddess again.

Ayus dressed himself in his royal attire, which was splendid white, adorned with gold and gems. He wore a crown of pearls on his head, and a necklace of rubies around his neck. He looked like a king again.

They then walked out of the chamber and went to the palace courtyard, where the other apsaras were waiting for Urvashi in their chariot drawn by swans. They were also accompanied by some gandharvas, who were carrying their musical instruments. They greeted Urvashi with joy and affection. They asked her how she had spent her night with Ayus. Urvashi told them that she had spent a wonderful night with Ayus, who was her son. They were surprised by Urvashi's revelation and congratulated her for finding her son. They also praised Ayus for being a great king and a noble man. They then invited Urvashi to join them in their chariot and fly back to heaven.

Urvashi agreed to join them in their chariot, but before that, she wanted to say goodbye to Ayus.

She turned to Ayus and said: "O Ayus, this is the moment of our farewell. I have to leave you now and fly back to heaven with my friends. But I will always remember you in my heart and pray for you from above. Please take care of yourself and your kingdom. Please follow dharma and uphold justice. Please be happy and successful."

Ayus said: "O Urvashi, this is the moment of our farewell. You have to leave me now and fly back to heaven with your friends. But I will always remember you in my heart and worship you from below. Please take care of yourself and your heaven. Please follow Indra's commands and serve him well. Please be happy and successful."

They then hugged each other one last time and kissed each other on their foreheads.

They then let go of each other's hands and stepped back.

Urvashi then climbed up the chariot with the other apsaras.

The gandharvas then played their instruments and sang a song of farewell.

The swans then flapped their wings and lifted the chariot into the air.

Urvashi then waved her hand at Ayus and said: "Goodbye, my son."

Ayus then waved his hand at Urvashi and said: "Goodbye, my mother."

They then watched each other until they disappeared from each other's sight.

Karna: A Noble Warrior's Fate and Betrayal

Karna was a noble warrior who fought for the Kauravas in the Kurukshetra war. He was the son of the sun god Surya and princess Kunti, but he did not know his true identity until the end of his life. He was abandoned by his mother at birth and raised by a charioteer and his wife. He faced many hardships and challenges in his life, but he also had many virtues and talents. He was loyal, generous, brave, skilled, and honourable. He was also cursed, betrayed, humiliated, and killed. He was a tragic hero who deserved a better fate.

This is his story.

Karna's Birth and Adoption

This story is in the Mahabharata, Vana Parva, Chapters 301-306 [1]

Kunti was the adopted daughter of King Kuntibhoja of Kunti Rashtra. She was a beautiful and virtuous princess who was well-versed in the scriptures. Once, a sage named Durvasa visited her father's palace and stayed there for a year. He was known for his temper and his curses, but he was also capable of granting boons to those who pleased him.

Kunti served him with devotion and care during his stay. She attended to his needs and followed his instructions without any complaint. Durvasa was impressed by her service and decided to reward her with a special boon. He gave her a mantra that could invoke any god and obtain a child from him.

Kunti was curious about the mantra and wanted to test it. She went to her room and chanted the mantra, invoking Surya, the sun god. To her surprise, Surya appeared before her in his radiant form. He told her that he had come to give her a son as per the mantra.

Kunti was shocked and scared. She told him that she had invoked him only out of curiosity and that she did not want a son from him. She begged him to go back to his abode and spare her from dishonour.

Surya told her that he could not go back without fulfilling the mantra. He said that if he did so, he would incur a curse from Durvasa and bring misfortune to both of them. He assured her that he would give her a son who would be equal to him in glory and splendour. He also promised her that she would not lose her virginity or reputation by bearing his son.

Kunti had no choice but to accept his offer. She agreed to have a son from him, but she asked him to grant her two boons. She asked him to make her son invulnerable by giving him divine armour and earrings at birth. She also asked him to make her son loyal and righteous by giving him a noble heart.

Surya granted her both boons and impregnated her with his power. He then disappeared from her sight.

Kunti soon realised that she was pregnant with Surya's son. She was terrified of the consequences of her act. She knew that she could not reveal her secret to anyone or face their wrath and scorn. She decided to hide her pregnancy until she delivered the child.

She gave birth to a son in secret at night. She saw that he was indeed endowed with a golden armour and earrings that shone like the sun. He was also handsome and strong like his father. She named him Karna, meaning "the one who is born with an armour".

She loved him dearly, but she also feared for his safety and future. She knew that she could not keep him with her or raise him as her own. She decided to abandon him in a river, hoping that someone would find him and adopt him.

She wrapped him in a cloth, placed him in a basket, and set him adrift in the river Aswa. She prayed to Surya to protect him and guide him to a good family.

She then returned to her room, crying silently for her lost son.

The basket floated down the river until it reached the city of Hastinapura, where King Dhritarashtra ruled over the Kuru clan. There lived a charioteer named Adhiratha, who worked for the king. He was married to Radha, who was barren and longed for a child.

One day, Adhiratha went to the river to fetch some water for his household. He saw the basket floating on the water and decided to check it out. He opened it and found a baby boy inside it. He was amazed by the boy's beauty and radiance. He also noticed his armour and earrings that sparkle like jewels.

He felt pity for the abandoned child and decided to adopt him as his own. He took him to his wife and showed him to her. Radha was overjoyed to see the child and embraced him with love. She thanked the gods for sending them a son.

They named him Vasusena, meaning "the one who is born with wealth". They also called him Radheya, meaning "the son of Radha". They raised him with affection and care, along with their other children.

Karna grew up in the charioteer's family, unaware of his true origin and destiny. He was happy and content with his life, but he also felt a sense of difference and isolation from others. He was aware that he was not a real son of Adhiratha and Radha, but an adopted one. He was also aware that he was not a real Kshatriya, but a Suta, a mixed caste of charioteers and poets.

He faced many difficulties and discrimination because of his caste and status. He was often mocked and insulted by his peers and elders. He was denied the opportunities and privileges that were given to the Kshatriyas. He was treated as an inferior and an outsider by society.

But he did not let these obstacles stop him from pursuing his dreams and passions. He had a strong will and a brave spirit. He had a keen interest and a natural talent in archery. He wanted to become a great archer and a warrior like his idols, Arjuna and Bhishma.

He practised archery with dedication and diligence, using whatever resources he could find. He made his own bow and arrows from bamboo and wood. He learned the basics of archery from his father and other charioteers. He also learned the art of warfare from the soldiers and generals who visited the king's palace.

He became proficient in archery and warfare, surpassing many of his peers and elders. He also developed other skills and qualities that made him a noble and admirable person. He was loyal, generous, brave, skilled, and honourable. He was also humble, polite, respectful, and grateful.

He was loved and respected by his family and friends, who supported him and encouraged him. He was also admired and praised by many people who recognized his talents and virtues.

He became a hero among the Sutas, who looked up to him as their leader and protector.

He became a legend among the Kshatriyas, who feared him as their rival and challenger.

He became Karna, the noble warrior who fought for his honour and glory.

When Karna grew up, he became a skilled archer and warrior, but he also faced many challenges and hardships because of his low caste and status. He was often mocked and insulted by his peers and elders, and denied the opportunities and privileges that were given to the Kshatriyas. He was treated as an inferior and an outsider by society.

He had a strong desire to learn the art of warfare from the best teachers, but he was rejected by Dronacharya, who only taught Kshatriyas. He then decided to learn from Parashurama, who only taught Brahmins. He disguised himself as a Brahmin and became Parashurama's disciple. He learned many secrets and skills from Parashurama, including the use of the Brahmastra, a powerful divine weapon. However, he was later cursed by Parashurama when his true identity was revealed. Parashurama cursed him that he would forget the Brahmastra when he needed it the most.

He also participated in Draupadi's swayamvara, where he impressed everyone with his archery skills. He was about to win Draupadi's hand, but he was stopped by Draupadi's brother, who questioned his caste and lineage. Draupadi also rejected him, calling him a suta-putra, or a son of a charioteer. He felt humiliated and angry by this insult.

He then became friends with Duryodhana, the eldest of the Kauravas, who appreciated his talents and virtues. Duryodhana made him the king of Anga, a province under his rule. Karna became loyal and grateful to Duryodhana, and supported him in his rivalry with the Pandavas. He also developed a personal enmity with Arjuna, the third Pandava, who was considered to be the greatest archer of his time.

He fought for the Kauravas in the Kurukshetra war, where he faced many difficulties and dangers. He was cursed by a Brahmin for killing his cow by mistake. He was also cursed by Indra, the father of Arjuna, who tricked him into giving away his divine armour and earrings that made him invulnerable. He was also insulted and abandoned by Shalya, his charioteer and uncle.

He finally met his death at the hands of Arjuna, who shot him with an arrow when his chariot wheel was stuck in the mud. Before dying, he learned from Kunti that she was his biological mother, and that he was the eldest brother of the Pandavas. He died with mixed feelings of sorrow and relief.

Karna's life was full of tragedy and glory. He was a noble warrior who fought for his honour and dignity. He was also a generous and righteous person who helped many people in need. He was admired and respected by many people who recognized his qualities and achievements.

One possible moral from the story is that one should not judge a person by their birth or caste, but by their character and actions. Karna was born as a son of a god, but he was abandoned by his mother and raised by a charioteer. He faced many hardships and discrimination because of his low caste and status. He was denied the respect and recognition that he deserved as a warrior and a prince. He was also betrayed and cursed by many people who envied or feared him. However, he did not let these obstacles stop him from pursuing his dreams and passions.

He became a skilled archer and warrior, who fought for his honour and dignity. He was also a generous and righteous person, who helped many people in need. He was admired and respected by many people who recognized his qualities and achievements.

Some ethics that one can learn from the story are:

- Be loyal to your friends and benefactors, who support you and encourage you. Karna was loyal to Duryodhana, who made him the king of Anga and treated him as an equal. He supported him in his rivalry with the Pandavas, even though he knew that they were his brothers.

- Be generous to the poor and needy, who depend on you and appreciate you. Karna was generous to anyone who asked him for anything, even if it meant giving away his own possessions or life. He gave away his divine armour and earrings to Indra, who disguised himself as a Brahmin and asked him for charity

- Be brave in the face of danger and adversity, who challenge you and test you. Karna was brave in every battle and every situation, even when he faced overwhelming odds or powerful enemies. He fought against Arjuna, Bhishma, Parashurama, and many other warriors, who were considered to be the best in their fields.

- Be skilled in your chosen field and profession, who inspire you and motivate you. Karna was skilled in archery and warfare, which were his passions and dreams. He learned from the best teachers, such as Parashurama, and practised with dedication and diligence. He became proficient in using various weapons and techniques, such as the Brahmastra.

- Be honourable in your conduct and behaviour, who define you and distinguish you. Karna was honourable in his words and deeds, even when he faced insults and humiliations. He never lied or cheated or broke his promises. He never harmed or killed anyone who was unarmed or helpless. He always followed the rules of war and the code of ethics.

Shakuntala and Dushyanta: A Forgotten Love Rekindled

Shakuntala was the daughter of the sage Vishwamitra and the apsara Menaka, who had abandoned her at birth. She was raised by the sage Kanva in his ashram, where she lived a simple and peaceful life. She was beautiful and virtuous, and loved by all the creatures of the forest.

Dushyanta was the king of Hastinapura, a powerful and prosperous kingdom. He was brave and generous, and respected by all his subjects. He loved hunting and adventure, and often roamed the lands with his army.

One day, Dushyanta was chasing a deer in the forest, when he came across the ashram of Kanva. He saw Shakuntala watering the plants, accompanied by her friends Anasuya and Priyamvada. He was struck by her beauty and grace, and felt a sudden attraction towards her.

He approached her and introduced himself as a hunter. He asked her about herself and her life in the ashram. Shakuntala was shy and modest, but also curious and friendly. She told him that she was the daughter of Kanva, who had adopted her as his own. She also told him about her love for nature and animals.

They talked for a while, and felt a mutual admiration and affection for each other. They exchanged smiles and glances, and felt their hearts beating faster.

Meanwhile, Kanva returned to the ashram after a long absence. He welcomed Dushyanta as his guest, and invited him to stay for some time. Dushyanta agreed, hoping to spend more time with Shakuntala.

During his stay, Dushyanta and Shakuntala fell in love with each other. They met secretly in the garden, where they expressed their feelings and shared their dreams. They also sang songs and recited poems that they had learned from each other.

One day, Dushyanta proposed to Shakuntala, saying that he wanted to marry her and make her his queen. Shakuntala accepted his proposal, saying that she wanted to be with him forever. They married according to the gandharva rites, which did not require any witnesses or ceremonies.

They spent some blissful days together, until Dushyanta had to return to his kingdom. He promised to come back soon for Shakuntala, and gave her his royal ring as a token of his love. He asked her to keep it safe until he returned.

Shakuntala bid him farewell with tears in her eyes, and waited eagerly for his return.

However, fate had other plans for them.

A few days later, a sage named Durvasa visited the ashram. He was known for his anger and his curses, but also for his power and wisdom. He expected to be greeted with respect and hospitality by everyone in the ashram.

Shakuntala was lost in her thoughts about Dushyanta, and did not notice Durvasa's arrival. She failed to greet him properly or offer him any service. Durvasa felt offended by her neglect, and cursed her that the person she was thinking of would forget her completely.

Shakuntala did not hear the curse being uttered by Durvasa, who left the ashram in a huff.

When Kanva learned about what had happened, he was worried about Shakuntala's fate. He decided to send her to Dushyanta's palace, hoping that he would recognize her as his wife.

He asked some of his disciples to accompany Shakuntala to Hastinapura, where Dushyanta ruled as king.

Shakuntala left the ashram with a heavy heart, but also with a hope of reuniting with her beloved husband.

She carried with her a precious gift: she was pregnant with Dushyanta's child.

On their way to Hastinapura, they had to cross a river by boat. As they were crossing the river, Shakuntala felt thirsty and asked for some water. One of the disciples gave her a cup of water from the river.

As she was drinking the water, she noticed something shiny in it. It was Dushyanta's ring, which had slipped from her finger into the water without her noticing it.

She tried to catch it before it sank into the depths of the river, but it was too late. The ring was gone forever.

She felt a pang of fear in her heart, as if she had lost something very important.

She did not know that she had lost more than just a ring.

She had lost her only hope of being remembered by Dushyanta.

The curse of Durvasa had taken effect.

When Shakuntala reached Hastinapura with her companions, she was shocked by what she saw.

Dushyanta did not recognize her at all.

He looked at her with indifference and suspicion, and asked her who she was and what she wanted from him.

Shakuntala was hurt and confused by his cold and rude behaviour. She told him that she was his wife, whom he had married in the forest. She showed him her belly, which was swollen with his child. She asked him to remember their love and their vows.

Dushyanta did not believe her words. He thought that she was a liar and a cheat, who was trying to trap him into a false marriage. He accused her of being an impostor and a seductress, who had come to ruin his reputation and his kingdom.

He ordered his guards to throw her out of his palace, and warned her never to come back again.

Shakuntala was devastated by his rejection and his insults. She felt as if her heart had been broken into pieces. She pleaded with him to listen to her and look into her eyes. She begged him to recall their happy moments and their sweet memories.

But Dushyanta did not listen to her or look at her. He turned away from her and dismissed her as a stranger.

He had forgotten her completely.

Shakuntala had no choice but to leave the palace with her companions, who were also shocked and saddened by Dushyanta's behaviour.

She left the palace with tears in her eyes, and a curse on her lips.

She cursed Dushyanta that he would suffer the same pain and sorrow that he had caused her. She cursed him that he would never find peace or happiness until he remembered her and accepted her as his wife.

She then left Hastinapura, never to return again.

She wandered in the forest, alone and hopeless.

She gave birth to a son in the forest, whom she named Sarvadamana, meaning "the one who subdues all". He was a brave and strong boy, who inherited his father's valour and his mother's virtue. He grew up in the wild, playing with animals and plants. He learned the skills of survival and warfare from nature itself.

He also learned the secrets of his birth and his destiny from his mother, who told him about his father and his kingdom.

She told him that he was the rightful heir of Hastinapura, and that he had to claim his throne someday.

She also told him that he had to forgive his father for his mistake, and reunite with him as his son.

She told him that he had to fulfil the prophecy of the gods, who had destined him to be the founder of a great dynasty.

She told him that he was Bharata, the ancestor of the Kurus.

Meanwhile, Dushyanta continued to rule over Hastinapura, but he was not happy or satisfied. He felt a void in his heart, which he could not fill with anything. He felt a guilt in his mind, which he could not erase with anything. He felt a restlessness in his soul, which he could not calm with anything.

He did not know what was wrong with him or what he was missing.

He did not know that he was missing Shakuntala and their son.

He did not know that he was missing his true love and his true heir.

He did not know that he was missing his true self.

One day, while hunting in the forest, he came across a boy who was playing with a lion cub. The boy was fearless and fierce, and he challenged Dushyanta to a fight. Dushyanta was impressed by the boy's courage and skill, and asked him who he was and where he came from.

The boy told him that he was Sarvadamana, the son of Shakuntala, who lived in the forest. He also told him that he was Bharata, the son of Dushyanta, who ruled over Hastinapura.

Dushyanta was stunned by the boy's words. He felt a flash of memory in his mind, and a surge of emotion in his heart. He remembered Shakuntala and their marriage in the forest. He remembered their love and their vows. He remembered their son and their ring.

He realised that he had forgotten them all because of a curse. He realised that he had wronged them all because of a mistake. He realised that he had lost them all because of a fate.

He felt ashamed and sorry for what he had done. He felt happy and proud for what they had become. He felt hopeful and eager for what they could be.

He embraced the boy as his son, and asked for his forgiveness. He also asked him to take him to Shakuntala, whom he wanted to see again.

The boy forgave him as his father, and agreed to take him to Shakuntala, whom he wanted to meet again.

They went together to Shakuntala's hut in the forest, where she lived alone with her sorrow.

I will try to continue the story for you based on Hindu mythology and Indian literature. Here is the part I have added:

Shakuntala saw them coming from afar, and recognized them both. She saw Dushyanta, her husband, whom she had loved and lost. She saw Bharata, her son, whom she had raised and cherished. She felt a mixture of joy and pain in her heart.

She ran towards them and embraced them both. She kissed Bharata on his forehead and thanked him for bringing Dushyanta to her. She then looked at Dushyanta with tears in her eyes and asked him why he had come to her.

Dushyanta told her that he had come to apologise for his mistake and to ask for her forgiveness. He told her that he had forgotten her and their son because of a curse, but that he had remembered them when he met Bharata in the forest. He told her that he loved her and wanted to be with her again.

Shakuntala listened to his words and felt a surge of emotion in her heart. She remembered their happy days together, and their sad parting. She remembered his rejection and his insults, and his repentance and his praises. She remembered their love and their vows, and their curse and their fate.

She forgave him as her husband, and agreed to be with him again.

They hugged each other and kissed each other on their lips.

They then went together to Hastinapura, where Dushyanta ruled as king.

He welcomed them with honour and joy, and introduced them to his people as his queen and his heir.

He also gave them gifts and jewels, and made them comfortable in his palace.

He then held a grand celebration for their reunion, where he invited all the sages, kings, gods, and apsaras.

He also performed a sacrifice for the welfare of all beings.

He then lived happily with Shakuntala and Bharata, who brought him peace and happiness.

He also ruled his kingdom well and protected his people from enemies.

He also followed dharma and upheld justice.

He became a great king and a noble man.

Shakuntala also lived happily with Dushyanta and Bharata, who gave her love and respect.

She also taught them the wisdom of the scriptures, and the beauty of nature.

She also helped them in their duties and affairs.

She also performed many charities and services for the needy.

She became a great queen and a noble woman.

Bharata also lived happily with Dushyanta and Shakuntala, who were his parents and teachers.

He also learned the skills of warfare and governance, and the virtues of courage and generosity.

He also proved himself in many battles and adventures.

He also expanded his kingdom and conquered many lands.

He also established a new dynasty that was named after him.

He became a great warrior and a noble king.

Shakuntala, Dushyanta, and Bharata were reunited by fate after being separated by fate. They were rekindled by love after being forgotten by love. They were blessed by the gods after being cursed by the gods.

They were happy together, until they left this world for the next one.

Love is stronger than fate, and can overcome any obstacle or hardship. Shakuntala and Dushyanta loved each other, but they were separated by a curse that made them forget each other. They suffered a lot of pain and sorrow, but they also kept their hope and faith. They were reunited by their son, who reminded them of their love. They forgive each other for their mistakes, and accept each other as their partners. They lived happily together, and became great rulers and parents. They showed that love can heal any wound, and can restore any memory.

Draupadi: A Fiery Woman's Struggles and Faith

Draupadi was a fiery woman who faced many struggles and hardships in her life, but also had a strong faith and devotion to Lord Krishna. She was the daughter of King Drupada of Panchala, and the wife of the five Pandava brothers: Yudhishthira, Bhima, Arjuna, Nakula, and Sahadeva. She was also the mother of five sons, one from each husband, who were known as the Upapandavas. She was one of the most beautiful and virtuous women in the world, and one of the five virgins (Panchakanya) whose names are believed to dispel sin when recited.

This is her story.

Draupadi's Birth and Marriage

This story is in the Mahabharata, Adi Parva, Chapters 158-190

Draupadi was not born in a normal way, but from a sacrificial fire that was performed by her father, King Drupada. Drupada wanted to take revenge on Dronacharya, the teacher of the Kauravas and the Pandavas, who had defeated him in a previous war and taken half of his kingdom. Drupada wanted to have a son who could kill Dronacharya, and a daughter who could marry Arjuna, the best archer among the Pandavas.

Drupada invited many sages and priests to perform a special fire sacrifice for him. He offered many gifts and prayers to the gods, and asked them to grant him his wish. The gods were pleased with his offerings and prayers, and decided to fulfil his desire.

From the fire emerged a beautiful girl with dark complexion and radiant eyes. She was dressed in red silk and adorned with jewels. She looked like a goddess herself. A heavenly voice announced that she was Draupadi, the daughter of Drupada, who would bring glory to her father and her husbands.

Drupada was overjoyed to see his daughter, and named her Krishnaa, meaning "the dark one". He also called her Panchali, meaning "the one from Panchala". He embraced her with love and pride, and thanked the gods for their blessing.

From the same fire also emerged a boy with fair complexion and bright eyes. He was dressed in yellow silk and armed with a bow and arrows. He looked like a warrior himself. A heavenly voice announced that he was Dhrishtadyumna, the son of Drupada, who would kill Dronacharya.

Drupada was equally happy to see his son, and named him Dhrishtadyumna, meaning "the one with splendid splendour". He also called him Dhrista, meaning "the bold one". He hugged him with affection and joy, and thanked the gods for their boon.

Drupada then raised his children with care and education. He taught them the art of warfare and governance, as well as the wisdom of the scriptures and culture. He also prepared them for their future roles and missions.

When Draupadi grew up into a young woman, she was renowned for her beauty, intelligence, and virtue. She was admired by many kings and princes who wanted to marry her. Drupada decided to hold a swayamvara for her, where she could choose her own husband from among the suitors.

He invited many kings and princes from different lands to participate in the swayamvara. He also set up a difficult test for them to prove their worthiness. He placed a golden fish on top of a pole, which had a revolving wheel attached to it. The fish had an eye that was visible through the wheel. The suitors had to shoot an arrow through the eye of the fish by looking at its reflection in a pool of water below.

Many suitors tried their luck at the test, but none of them could hit the target. Some missed the fish completely, some hit the wheel instead of the eye, some broke their bows or arrows in frustration. They all failed miserably.

Among the suitors were also Karna, the friend of Duryodhana, the eldest of the Kauravas; and Arjuna, disguised as a Brahmin along with his brothers Yudhishthira and Bhima. Karna was confident that he could pass the test, as he was an expert archer who had learned from Parashurama himself. He took up his bow and arrow, and aimed at the fish.

However, before he could release his arrow, Draupadi stopped him. She said that she did not want to marry a suta-putra (son of a charioteer), as Karna was believed to be. She said that she only wanted to marry a Kshatriya (warrior caste) of noble birth and lineage. She insulted Karna and asked him to leave the arena.

Karna felt humiliated and angry by Draupadi's words. He knew that he was not a suta-putra, but the son of Surya, the sun god, and Kunti, the mother of the Pandavas. He also knew that he was the elder brother of the Pandavas, though they did not know it. He wanted to reveal his true identity and challenge Draupadi, but he restrained himself. He respected the rules of the swayamvara and withdrew from the contest.

Arjuna, who was watching the scene, felt sorry for Karna. He also felt a spark of attraction towards Draupadi, who had impressed him with her beauty and courage. He decided to try his luck at the test, as he was confident that he could pass it. He had learned archery from Dronacharya himself, and had also received many divine weapons from various gods.

He took up his bow and arrow, and aimed at the fish. He looked at its reflection in the water, and calculated the angle and distance. He then released his arrow with perfect precision and skill. The arrow flew through the air and pierced through the eye of the fish, making it fall to the ground.

The crowd erupted in cheers and applause, as they witnessed Arjuna's feat. They praised him for his archery and congratulated him for winning Draupadi's hand.

Draupadi was also amazed by Arjuna's skill and charmed by his appearance. She felt a surge of love and admiration for him. She walked towards him with a garland of flowers in her hand, ready to accept him as her husband.

However, before she could reach him, she heard a voice in her ear. It was Lord Krishna, who was her friend and protector. He told her that Arjuna was not alone, but had four brothers with him. He told her that she had to marry all five of them, as they were destined to be her husbands.

Draupadi was shocked and confused by Krishna's words. She asked him how it was possible or proper for her to marry five men at once. She asked him what people would say or think about her.

Krishna told her not to worry or fear about anything. He told her that it was all part of a divine plan, which had a deeper meaning and purpose. He told her that she was not an ordinary woman, but a goddess incarnate. He told her that she had been born from fire to help him establish dharma (righteousness) on earth. He told her that she had to marry the five Pandavas, who were also gods incarnate. He told her that they were all part of a cosmic drama, which would end in a great war.

He also told her that this was not the first time that she had married five men. He told her that in her previous life, she was Nalayani, the wife of Sage Maudgalya. She had asked him for a boon to physically mate with him in five different forms, which he had granted. As a result, she had been cursed by Lord Shiva to have five husbands in her next life.

He also told her that this was not the first time that the Pandavas had married one woman. He told them that in their previous life, they were Indra's sons who had married Ahalya, the wife of Sage Gautama. They had done so at Indra's request, who wanted to test Ahalya's fidelity. As a result, they had been cursed by Gautama to share one wife in their next life.

Krishna then asked Draupadi to trust him and follow his advice. He assured her that he would always be with her and guide her through all difficulties and dangers. He asked her to be brave and virtuous, and fulfil her duty and destiny.

Draupadi listened to Krishna's words and felt a sense of faith and surrender in her heart. She believed that he knew what was best for her and everyone else. She agreed to marry all five Pandavas, as he had suggested.

She then reached Arjuna and garlanded him as her husband. She also looked at his brothers Yudhishthira, Bhima, Nakula, and Sahadeva with respect and affection. She accepted them as her husbands too.

The Pandavas were also surprised and puzzled by Krishna's words. They did not know how or why they had to marry one woman together. They also did not know how their mother Kunti would react to this situation.

They decided to take Draupadi to their mother first, before announcing their marriage to anyone else.

They left the swayamvara hall with Draupadi and their friends Krishna and Balarama.

They reached their hut where Kunti was waiting for them.

They also informed Drupada about their marriage, who was initially angry and shocked by their decision. He did not approve of his daughter marrying five men at once, especially when one of them was Arjuna, who had defeated him in a previous war. He also did not like the fact that they were living as Brahmins in disguise, and that they had no kingdom or wealth of their own.

However, when he learned that this was a divine plan, and that Krishna was involved in it, he changed his mind. He realised that his daughter and her husbands were not ordinary people, but gods incarnate. He also realised that they had a great destiny ahead of them, which would change the course of history. He decided to accept them as his son-in-laws, and to support them in their cause.

He then invited them to his palace, where he welcomed them with honour and joy. He also gave them many gifts and jewels, and made them comfortable in his palace.

He then held a grand celebration for their marriage, where he invited many sages, kings, gods, and apsaras.

He also performed a sacrifice for the welfare of all beings.

He then lived happily with Draupadi and her husbands, who brought him peace and happiness.

He also helped them in their duties and affairs.

He also followed dharma and upheld justice.

He became a great king and a noble father.

Draupadi also lived happily with her husbands, who loved her and respected her. She also loved them equally and sincerely, and fulfilled her duties as a wife. She also taught them the wisdom of the scriptures, and the beauty of nature.

She also helped them in their duties and affairs.

She also performed many charities and services for the needy.

She became a great queen and a noble woman.

The Pandavas also lived happily with Draupadi, who was their wife and friend. They also learned the skills of warfare and governance, and the virtues of courage and generosity. They also proved themselves in many battles and adventures.

They also expanded their kingdom and conquered many lands.

They also established a new dynasty that was named after them.

They became great warriors and noble kings.

Draupadi, Drupada, and the Pandavas were happy together, until they faced a new challenge from their cousins, the Kauravas.

The Kauravas were the cousins of the Pandavas, who were the sons of Dhritarashtra, the blind king of Hastinapura. They were a hundred in number, led by Duryodhana, who was the eldest and the most wicked. They were jealous and hateful of the Pandavas, who were more virtuous and successful than them. They wanted to take away their kingdom and wealth, and to humiliate and harm them.

They plotted and schemed against the Pandavas, and tried to kill them in various ways. They poisoned Bhima, who was saved by Hanuman, his brother from another mother. They set fire to their house, which they escaped through a secret tunnel. They challenged them to a game of dice, which they rigged with the help of Shakuni, their uncle and a master of deception.

In the game of dice, Yudhishthira, the eldest Pandava, who was addicted to gambling, lost everything he had: his kingdom, his wealth, his brothers, and even Draupadi. Duryodhana then ordered his brother Dushasana to drag Draupadi to the court and disrobe her in front of everyone.

Draupadi was horrified and humiliated by this act. She prayed to Lord Krishna for help and protection. Krishna heard her prayers and performed a miracle. He made her saree endless, so that no matter how much Dushasana pulled it, he could not uncover her.

Draupadi was saved by Krishna's grace, but she was also angry and hurt by her husbands' failure to defend her. She cursed the Kauravas for their wickedness, and vowed to take revenge on them. She also asked her husbands to fight for their rights and honour, and to reclaim their kingdom from their enemies.

The Pandavas were also ashamed and enraged by what had happened. They challenged the Kauravas for another game of dice, where the loser would have to go into exile for twelve years, followed by one year of living incognito. If they were discovered during the thirteenth year, they would have to repeat the cycle.

The Kauravas agreed to this challenge, confident that they would win again. However, this time, Yudhishthira won the game with Krishna's help. He then asked the Kauravas to keep their promise and give back their kingdom.

The Kauravas refused to do so, saying that they had won it fair and square. They also said that they would not let them live in peace or happiness. They said that they would wage war against them until they were destroyed.

The Pandavas realised that there was no hope of a peaceful settlement with the Kauravas. They decided to prepare for war against them, with Krishna as their ally and guide.

They then left Hastinapura with Draupadi and their friends, and went into exile for twelve years.

They faced many hardships and dangers during their exile, but they also had many adventures and achievements.

They met many sages and kings who helped them and taught them.

They also acquired many weapons and allies who supported them.

They also performed many sacrifices and charities for the welfare of all beings.

They also followed dharma and upheld justice.

They became stronger and wiser during their exile.

Draupadi also faced many hardships and dangers during her exile, but she also had a strong faith and devotion to Krishna. She also supported her husbands in their trials and tribulations.

She also taught them the wisdom of the scriptures, and the beauty of nature.

She also helped them in their duties and affairs.

She also performed many charities and services for the needy.

She became more virtuous and noble during her exile.

After twelve years of exile, they entered into the thirteenth year, where they had to live incognito without being recognized by anyone.

They chose to live in the kingdom of Virata, where Yudhishthira disguised himself as a Brahmin named Kanka; Bhima as a cook named Vallabha; Arjuna as a eunuch named Brihannala; Nakula as a horse-trainer named Granthika; Sahadeva as a cowherd named Tantripala; and Draupadi as a maid named Sairandhri.

They served King Virata and his family with loyalty and skill, without revealing their true identity or purpose.

However, they also faced many troubles and risks during their stay in Virata's kingdom.

Draupadi was harassed by Kichaka, the brother-in-law of Virata, who was attracted by her beauty and wanted to marry her. He tried to seduce her several times, but she rejected him firmly. He then tried to force himself on her, but she resisted him bravely. She then asked Bhima for help, who killed Kichaka in a fierce fight.

The Kauravas also attacked Virata's kingdom, hoping to find the Pandavas and expose them. They stole Virata's cattle, and challenged him to a war. The Pandavas came to Virata's rescue, and fought against the Kauravas in disguise. They defeated them and recovered the cattle, without being recognized by them.

The Pandavas also revealed their true identity to Virata and his family, who were surprised and delighted by their presence. They thanked them for their service and friendship, and offered them their support and alliance.

They then completed their thirteenth year of exile, without being discovered by the Kauravas.

They then claimed their right to their kingdom, and asked the Kauravas to return it to them.

The Kauravas refused to do so, saying that they had failed to complete their exile, as they had been seen by them during the war with Virata.

They also said that they would not give up their kingdom or wealth, and that they would fight against them until they were destroyed.

The Pandavas realised that there was no hope of a peaceful settlement with the Kauravas. They decided to wage war against them, with Krishna as their ally and guide.

They then left Virata's kingdom with Draupadi and their friends, and went to Kurukshetra, where the great war was about to begin.

Draupadi's life after the war was not very happy or peaceful. She had lost her father, her brothers, and her five sons in the war. She also had to witness the death of many of her friends and relatives, who had fought on both sides. She was grief-stricken and depressed by the loss of so many lives.

She resumed her role as the empress of Hastinapura, along with her husbands, who ruled as joint kings. She performed her duties as a queen and a mother, and tried to console and comfort her husbands and their other wives. She also helped in the reconstruction and administration of the kingdom, which had suffered a lot of damage and chaos due to the war.

She also maintained her devotion to Lord Krishna, who was her friend and protector. She prayed to him for guidance and solace, and thanked him for saving her from many dangers and difficulties. She also followed his teachings and advice, and tried to uphold dharma (righteousness) and justice.

However, she was not satisfied or content with her life. She felt a void in her heart, which she could not fill with anything. She felt a guilt in her mind, which she could not erase with anything. She felt a restlessness in her soul, which she could not calm with anything.

She did not know what was wrong with her or what she was missing.

She did not know that she was missing Krishna, who had left this world soon after the war.

She did not know that she was missing her true love and her true lord.

She did not know that she was missing her true self.

After ruling for 36 years, she decided to retire to the Himalayas along with her husbands. She wanted to renounce the worldly pleasures and attachments, and seek spiritual liberation. She wanted to end her cycle of birth and death, and attain moksha (salvation).

She left Hastinapura with tears in her eyes, and a hope in her heart.

She walked towards the Himalayas with courage and faith.

However, fate had other plans for her.

On their way to the Himalayas, they faced many hardships and obstacles. They had to cross many rivers, mountains, forests, and deserts. They also had to face many wild animals, robbers, and demons. They also had to endure hunger, thirst, cold, heat, fatigue, and pain.

They also had to face death.

One by one, they started falling down and dying on the way. First Sahadeva died, then Nakula, then Arjuna, then Bhima. Each time one of them died, Draupadi cried out in agony and grief. She asked Yudhishthira why they were dying before her.

Yudhishthira told her that each of them had a flaw or a sin that caused their death. Sahadeva died because he was proud of his wisdom. Nakula died because he was vain about his beauty. Arjuna died because he was arrogant about his skills. Bhima died because he was greedy for food.

Draupadi asked Yudhishthira what was her flaw or sin that would cause her death.

Yudhishthira told her that she loved Arjuna more than the other four husbands.

Draupadi was shocked and hurt by his words. She said that she loved all of them equally and sincerely. She said that she never discriminated among them or favoured anyone over the others.

Yudhishthira said that he knew that she loved all of them, but he also knew that she loved Arjuna more than the others. He said that this was natural and human, but it was also partial and unfair.

He then left her behind and continued his journey.

Draupadi felt abandoned and betrayed by Yudhishthira's words and actions. She felt as if her heart had been broken into pieces. She fell down on the ground and died.

She then left this world for the next one.

Vidura: A Wise Advisor's Teachings on Dharma

Vidura was a wise and virtuous man who served as the prime minister of the Kuru kingdom. He was the half-brother of Dhritarashtra and Pandu, the kings of Hastinapura, and the uncle of the Pandavas and the Kauravas, who fought each other in the great war of Kurukshetra. Vidura was born from the sage Vyasa and a maid named Parishrami, who was sent by the queen Ambika to mate with Vyasa. Ambika was afraid of Vyasa's appearance and had closed her eyes when she was with him, resulting in the birth of the blind Dhritarashtra. Her sister Ambalika had turned pale with fear when she saw Vyasa, giving birth to the pale Pandu. Vidura, however, was born from a woman who had no fear of Vyasa, and thus he inherited his father's wisdom and righteousness. Some say that Vidura was an incarnation of Yama, the god of death and justice, who was cursed by a sage named Mandavya for punishing him unjustly

Vidura was respected by everyone for his knowledge and integrity. He was well-versed in the scriptures and the laws of dharma, which means the moral order that sustains the universe and human society. He always spoke the truth and advised his brothers and nephews to follow their dharma, or duty, according to their roles and stages of life. He also warned them of the consequences of adharma, or unrighteousness, which leads to chaos and suffering. Vidura was especially fond of the Pandavas, who were virtuous and brave, unlike their cousins, the Kauravas, who were wicked and cruel. He often helped them in times of trouble and guided them with his teachings.

One day, Vidura decided to visit his nephew Yudhishthira, the eldest of the Pandavas, who was living in exile in the forest with his brothers and wife Draupadi. The Pandavas had lost their kingdom and wealth to the Kauravas in a game of dice, which was rigged by their evil cousin Duryodhana with the help of his uncle Shakuni. Vidura had tried to stop Yudhishthira from playing the game, but he had not listened to him. Vidura had also protested against the humiliation of Draupadi, who was dragged to the court by Duryodhana's brother Dushasana and insulted by Duryodhana himself. Vidura had rebuked Duryodhana for his wickedness and reminded him of his dharma as a king and a kinsman. But Duryodhana had ignored him and called him ungrateful. Dhritarashtra, who loved his son blindly, had also remained silent and did not stop his son's misdeeds

Vidura felt sorry for his nephews and wanted to console them and give them some advice. He reached their hut in the forest and greeted them warmly. The Pandavas were happy to see him and welcomed him with respect and affection. They offered him some fruits and water and asked him about his well-being. Vidura said that he was fine but he was worried about them. He asked them how they were coping with their hardships and what they were doing in their exile.

Yudhishthira said that they were living peacefully in the forest, following the rules of dharma as prescribed for their stage of life as ascetics. He said that they were spending their time in meditation, prayer, charity, service, study, and self-control. He said that they had forgiven their enemies and harboured no ill-will towards them. He said that they were waiting for their exile to end so that they could reclaim their kingdom peacefully or fight for it if necessary.

Vidura praised Yudhishthira for his patience and piety. He said that he was proud of him for being a true follower of dharma. He said that dharma is not only a set of rules or duties but also a way of life that leads to happiness and liberation. He said that dharma is based on four principles: truth (satya), non-violence (ahimsa), purity (shaucha), and detachment (vairagya). He said that these principles are universal and applicable to all beings at all times.

Vidura then told Yudhishthira some stories from his own life and from the lives of other great people who had exemplified these principles in different situations. He said that these stories would illustrate how dharma can be practised in various circumstances and how it can help one overcome difficulties and achieve success. He said that these stories would also teach some valuable lessons and morals that would guide Yudhishthira and his brothers in their future endeavours.

The following are some of the stories that Vidura told Yudhishthira:

The Story of Satyakama Jabala

Vidura said that truth is the foundation of dharma and the highest virtue. He said that truth means not only speaking what is factual but also being honest with oneself and others. He said that truth gives one strength, courage, and clarity. He said that truth also leads to knowledge, which is the ultimate goal of human life.

Vidura then narrated the story of Satyakama Jabala, a young boy who wanted to study the Vedas, the sacred scriptures of the Hindus. Satyakama lived with his mother Jabala, who was a maid and had no idea who his father was. She had served many men in her life and did not remember who had fathered her son. Satyakama was curious about his lineage and asked his mother about it. Jabala told him the truth and said that she did not know who his father was. She said that he should call himself Satyakama Jabala, after his own name and hers.

Satyakama was not ashamed of his mother's honesty and accepted her answer. He then decided to go to a sage named Haridrumata Gautama, who was a renowned teacher of the Vedas. He approached the sage and asked him to accept him as his student. The sage asked him about his family and lineage, as it was customary to do so before admitting a student. Satyakama told him the truth and said that he did not know who his father was. He said that he was Satyakama Jabala, the son of Jabala, a maid.

The sage was impressed by Satyakama's honesty and sincerity. He said that he had never heard such a truthful answer from anyone before. He said that only a true brahmin, a person of the highest caste and learning, could speak such a truth without fear or shame. He said that Satyakama had proved himself to be a brahmin by his character and not by his birth. He accepted him as his student and taught him the Vedas.

Satyakama became a diligent and devoted student. He learned everything that the sage taught him and followed his instructions faithfully. One day, the sage asked him to take four hundred cows to the forest and tend them until they became a thousand. He said that this was part of his training and that he would learn something valuable from it.

Satyakama obeyed the sage and took the cows to the forest. He lived there for many years, taking care of the cows and practising meditation. He did not return until the cows became a thousand. On his way back, he met four different beings: a bull, a fire, a swan, and a diver bird. Each of them taught him a part of the supreme knowledge called Brahman, which is the essence of everything in the universe.

When Satyakama reached the sage's ashram, he greeted him respectfully and told him what he had learned from the four beings. The sage was amazed by Satyakama's wisdom and said that he had attained the highest knowledge of Brahman. He said that he had nothing more to teach him and that he had become his equal. He blessed him and praised him for being a true seeker of truth.

Vidura concluded the story by saying that Satyakama Jabala was an example of how truth can lead one to knowledge and liberation. He said that Satyakama Jabala's story was a lesson for Dhritarashtra, who was blinded by his attachment to his sons and his throne. He said that Dhritarashtra should follow the path of truth and righteousness, and not let his greed and pride ruin his life and the lives of others. He said that by being truthful, Dhritarashtra could still save himself and his kingdom from destruction. He urged him to listen to his advice and act wisely.

Some other stories that Vidura told Yudhishthira are:

- The story of the crane and the mongoose: Vidura told this story to warn Yudhishthira about the danger of trusting Duryodhana, who was like a crane pretending to be a friend but actually waiting for an opportunity to kill him. He said that once there was a crane who befriended a mongoose and invited him to his home. He said that the crane had a hidden intention of feeding the mongoose to his children, who were hungry. He said that the mongoose realised the crane's plot and killed him and his children instead. He said that this story showed how the wicked are destroyed by their own schemes.

- The story of the lion and the hare: Vidura told this story to encourage Yudhishthira to use his intelligence and courage to defeat Duryodhana, who was like a powerful lion terrorising the forest. He said that once there was a lion who killed and ate all the animals in the forest, except for a hare. He said that the hare decided to end the lion's tyranny by tricking him into jumping into a well, where he saw his own reflection and thought it was another lion. He said that the hare told the lion that there was another lion in the well who had challenged him for his territory. He said that the lion became furious and leaped into the well, only to drown himself. He said that this story showed how the wise can overcome the strong by their cleverness.

- The story of the king and the ascetic: Vidura told this story to teach Yudhishthira about the value of detachment and renunciation. He said that once there was a king who was very rich and powerful, but also very unhappy and dissatisfied. He said that he met an ascetic who was very poor and humble, but also very happy and content. He said that the king asked the ascetic how he could be so happy with nothing, while he himself was so miserable with everything. He said that the ascetic replied that he had nothing to lose or fear, while the king had everything to lose or fear. He said that the ascetic advised the king to give up his attachment to his wealth and power, and seek the true happiness of the self. He said that this story showed how attachment leads to sorrow, while detachment leads to joy.

Vidura continued his story by saying that Dhritarashtra did not heed his words and remained stubborn and blind. He said that Dhritarashtra's sons, led by the wicked Duryodhana, plotted against their cousins, the Pandavas, who were the rightful heirs to the throne. He said that they cheated the Pandavas in a game of dice and exiled them to the forest for twelve years, followed by one year of disguise. He said that they also tried to kill them several times, but failed due to the protection of Lord Krishna, who was the friend and guide of the Pandavas. Vidura said that after the period of exile was over, the Pandavas returned to claim their share of the kingdom, but Duryodhana refused to give them even a needlepoint of land. He said that this led to the great war of Kurukshetra, where the two sides fought for eighteen days. He said that in this war, all the sons of Dhritarashtra were killed, along with many other kings and warriors.

He said that Dhritarashtra himself lost his sight completely when he hugged the body of his eldest son, Duryodhana, who was crushed by the mace of Bhima, one of the Pandavas. Vidura said that after the war, Dhritarashtra realised his folly and regretted his actions. He said that he renounced his throne and went to the forest with his wife Gandhari and his sister-in-law Kunti, who were also grieving for their sons. He said that there they lived a life of penance and peace, until they died in a forest fire. He said that Dhritarashtra's story was a tragedy of how untruth can lead one to sorrow and bondage. He said that Dhritarashtra's story was a warning for those who follow the path of adharma, or unrighteousness.

Vidura continued his story by saying that while he was narrating the events of the war to Dhritarashtra, he was assisted by Sanjaya, who had the gift of divine vision granted by Vyasa. He said that Sanjaya could see everything that was happening on the battlefield, as if he was present there. He said that Sanjaya also had the power to hear the conversations of the warriors, and to understand their thoughts and feelings. He said that Sanjaya was a loyal and wise advisor, who did not hide anything from Dhritarashtra, even if it was unpleasant or painful. He said that Sanjaya also gave his own opinions and insights, based on his knowledge and experience. He said that Sanjaya was a true friend and well-wisher of Dhritarashtra, who tried to console him and guide him in his moments of grief and despair.

Vidura said that Sanjaya was the narrator of the Bhagavad Gita, the sacred dialogue between Krishna and Arjuna, which revealed the essence of dharma, karma, and bhakti. He said that Sanjaya was blessed to witness this divine discourse, which enlightened his mind and soul. He said that Sanjaya shared this wisdom with Dhritarashtra, hoping that he would learn from it and change his ways. He said that Sanjaya also described the various manifestations of Krishna's cosmic form, which amazed and awed him. He said that Sanjaya was a devotee of Krishna, who praised him as the supreme lord and protector of the world.

Vidura said that Sanjaya's role in the Mahabharata was very important and unique. He said that Sanjaya was not just a messenger or a reporter, but a visionary and a teacher. He said that Sanjaya was a witness to history, a chronicler of destiny, and a transmitter of truth. He said that Sanjaya's words were like a mirror, reflecting the reality of the war and its consequences. He said that Sanjaya's voice was like a lamp, illuminating the path of righteousness and liberation.

These are some of the teachings of Vidura: The wise advisor in the courtyard of Dhritarashtra.

Bhishma: A Loyal Warrior's Vow and Sacrifice

<u>Birth</u>

Long ago, there lived a king named Shantanu, who ruled over the kingdom of Hastinapura. He was a wise and just ruler, loved by his people and respected by his enemies. One day, he went to the banks of the river Ganga to enjoy the beauty of nature. There, he saw a woman of unparalleled grace and charm, who was none other than the goddess Ganga herself. He was instantly smitten by her and asked her to marry him.

She agreed, but on one condition: he would never question her actions or interfere with her decisions, no matter what she did. If he ever broke this promise, she would leave him forever. Shantanu agreed and they got married.

Soon, Ganga gave birth to a son, who was named Devavrata. He was a handsome and brave boy, endowed with divine qualities. However, as soon as he was born, Ganga took him to the river and drowned him. Shantanu was shocked and grieved, but he did not say anything, remembering his promise. This happened seven more times, and each time Ganga killed their son in the same way. Shantanu could not bear it any longer and finally asked her why she was doing this. Ganga then revealed her secret: she was cursed by a sage named Vasishtha to be the mother of eight Vasus, who were celestial beings that had stolen his cow Kamadhenu.

The sage had cursed them to be born as humans and suffer the consequences of their actions. Ganga had agreed to be their mother on the condition that she would free them from their human birth as soon as they were born. The eighth son, however, was Prabhasa, the leader of the Vasus, who had instigated the theft. He had to live a longer life on earth as a punishment for his crime.

Ganga then told Shantanu that she had to leave him, as he had broken his promise. She also said that she would return their eighth son to him when he grew up. She then took the boy with her and disappeared into the river.

Shantanu was heartbroken and lonely. He missed his wife and son terribly. He devoted himself to his duties as a king and tried to forget his sorrow.

Years passed by, and one day Shantanu went hunting in the forest. There, he saw a young man fighting a group of bandits single-handedly. He was amazed by his skill and courage and decided to help him. Together, they defeated the bandits and drove them away. Shantanu then asked the young man who he was and where he came from. The young man said that he was Devavrata, the son of Ganga and Shantanu himself.

Shantanu was overjoyed to see his long-lost son and embraced him warmly. He asked him how he had learned such martial arts and where he had been all these years. Devavrata said that Ganga had taken him to various sages and teachers who had taught him everything from archery to astronomy, from politics to philosophy. He said that he had mastered all the arts and sciences and had become an expert in warfare and statecraft. He also said that Ganga had told him about his father and his kingdom and had sent him back to him.

Shantanu was proud of his son and took him back to Hastinapura with him. He introduced him to his courtiers and subjects, who welcomed him with respect and admiration. He declared him as his heir-apparent and gave him the name Bhishma, which means "the terrible" or "the one who undertakes a terrible vow". He also gave him a boon that he could choose his own time of death.

Bhishma became the crown prince of Hastinapura and served his father faithfully. He was loved by all for his virtues and valour.

Vow

Some time later, Shantanu went to the banks of the river Yamuna to enjoy the beauty of nature. There, he saw a woman of exquisite beauty, who was the daughter of the king of Kashi. Her name was Satyavati, and she was also known as Matsyagandha, or "the one who smells like fish ", because she was born from a fish and had a fishy odour. She was a ferry woman who used to take people across the river in her boat.

Shantanu was instantly smitten by her and asked her to marry him. She agreed, but on one condition: her father would only give her hand to him if he promised that her son would inherit the throne of Hastinapura, instead of Bhishma. Shantanu was shocked and saddened by this demand. He could not agree to it, as it would be unfair to his loyal and deserving son. He also could not tell Satyavati the reason for his refusal, as it would reveal his previous marriage with Ganga and his boon to Bhishma. He decided to leave her and return to his palace.

However, he could not forget her and became depressed and restless. He lost interest in his duties and pleasures and spent his days in sorrow.

Bhishma noticed his father's condition and asked him what was troubling him. Shantanu tried to hide his feelings, but Bhishma persisted and finally got the truth out of him. He learned about Satyavati and her father's condition.

Bhishma was moved by his father's love and decided to sacrifice his own happiness for his sake. He went to Kashi and met Satyavati's father. He told him that he had come to ask for Satyavati's hand for his father. He also said that he was ready to renounce his right to the throne and make Satyavati's son the heir-apparent. He also said that he would never marry or have children of his own, so that there would be no competition or conflict among the descendants of Shantanu and Satyavati. He took a solemn vow, or pratigna, in front of the gods and sages, that he would remain celibate and loyal to his father and his kingdom for his entire life.

This vow was so terrible and unprecedented that it shook the heavens and the earth. The gods showered flowers on Bhishma and praised him for his devotion and courage. They also gave him another boon: he would be invincible in battle and no one could kill him except himself.

Satyavati's father was impressed by Bhishma's vow and agreed to give his daughter to Shantanu. He also gave Bhishma a new name: Bhishma Pitamaha, or "the grand sire of the Kurus", as he would be the ancestor of both the Pandavas and the Kauravas, who were the main protagonists of the Mahabharata.

Bhishma then brought Satyavati to Hastinapura and presented her to Shantanu. Shantanu was overjoyed to see her and thanked Bhishma for his sacrifice. He married Satyavati and made her his queen.

Bhishma became the guardian and protector of Hastinapura and its people. He served his father and stepmother faithfully. He also trained Satyavati's sons, Chitrangada and Vichitravirya, in martial arts and statecraft.

War

After Shantanu's death, Chitrangada became the king of Hastinapura. He was a brave and powerful ruler, but he was also arrogant and reckless. He challenged a Gandharva, or a celestial musician, who had the same name as him, to a duel. The Gandharva accepted the challenge and killed Chitrangada in the battle.

Bhishma then became the regent of Hastinapura and looked after Vichitravirya, who was still a young boy. He also arranged his marriage with two princesses of Kashi, Ambika and Ambalika, whom he had abducted from their swayamvara, or self-choice ceremony, where they were supposed to choose their husbands from among the suitors. He did this to fulfil Satyavati's wish of having a strong and royal lineage for her son.

However, Vichitravirya died soon after his marriage, without leaving any children. Satyavati was worried about the future of her family and asked Bhishma to marry one of the widows and produce an heir for the throne. Bhishma refused, saying that he had taken a vow of celibacy and could not break it. He also said that he had no desire for the throne or the pleasures of life.

Satyavati then remembered that she had another son from before her marriage with Shantanu. His name was Vyasa, and he was a sage and a poet, who had composed the Mahabharata. She had given birth to him when she was a young girl, after being seduced by a wandering sage named Parashara. She had kept this secret from everyone, except Bhishma, who had known about it and respected her for it.

She asked Bhishma to bring Vyasa to Hastinapura and persuade him to father children with Ambika and Ambalika, using a custom called niyoga, or levirate marriage, where a brother or a relative of a deceased man can impregnate his widow to continue his lineage. Bhishma agreed and went to find Vyasa.

He found him in his hermitage in the forest and told him about his mother's request. Vyasa agreed to help, but warned Bhishma that his children would not be ordinary. He said that they would be influenced by the circumstances of their conception and would have different qualities and destinies.

Bhishma then brought Vyasa to Hastinapura and introduced him to Satyavati. She was happy to see her son and thanked him for his help. She then asked Ambika and Ambalika to prepare themselves for meeting Vyasa.

The next day, Ambika was the first to go to Vyasa's chamber. She was frightened by his appearance and demeanour. He had long and matted hair, dark and rough skin, piercing eyes, and a stern expression. He smelled like smoke and herbs. He wore a deer skin and carried a staff. He looked like a wild man from the forest. She closed her eyes in fear when he approached her.

Vyasa noticed this and became angry. He said that because she had closed her eyes, she would give birth to a blind son. He then left her chamber.

The next day, Ambalika was the second to go to Vyasa's chamber. She was also scared by his appearance and demeanour. She turned pale when he approached her.

Vyasa noticed this and became annoyed. He said that because she had turned pale, she would give birth to a pale son. He then left her chamber.

Satyavati was disappointed by the results of the niyoga. She asked Vyasa to try again with one of the widows. Vyasa agreed, but said that he would not come back for another year.

The next year, Vyasa came back to Hastinapura. Satyavati asked Ambika to go to his chamber again. However, Ambika was too afraid to face him again. She sent her maid instead, who was loyal and brave. She disguised herself as Ambika and went to Vyasa's chamber.

Vyasa noticed this and became pleased. He said that because she had been honest and respectful, she would give birth to a wise son. He then left her chamber.

In due course of time, Ambika gave birth to a blind son, who was named Dhritarashtra. Ambalika gave birth to a pale son, who was named Pandu. The maid gave birth to a wise son, who was named Vidura.

Bhishma raised them as his own nephews and taught them everything he knew. He also appointed Vidura as his chief minister and adviser.

Dhritarashtra became the king of Hastinapura, as he was the eldest son of Vichitravirya. However, he could not rule directly because of his blindness. Pandu became the commander-in-chief of the army and the de facto ruler. Vidura became the voice of reason and justice in the court.

Dhritarashtra married Gandhari, the princess of Gandhara, who blindfolded herself to share his blindness. She gave birth to a hundred sons, who were called the Kauravas. The eldest of them was Duryodhana, who was ambitious and wicked.

Pandu married Kunti, the princess of Kunti, and Madri, the princess of Madra. He had five sons, who were called the Pandavas. They were Yudhishthira, Bhima, Arjuna, Nakula, and Sahadeva. They were virtuous and heroic.

The Pandavas and the Kauravas grew up together in Hastinapura, but they did not get along well. They were always competing and fighting with each other. The Kauravas were jealous of the Pandavas and tried to harm them in various ways. The Pandavas were loyal to their elders and tried to avoid conflict.

Bhishma tried to maintain peace and harmony among them, but he could not prevent the growing animosity and rivalry between them. He also could not intervene in their affairs, as he had vowed to obey the king and his successors.

The situation worsened when Pandu died in the forest, where he had gone hunting. He had accidentally killed a sage named Kindama, who had cursed him that he would die if he ever approached a woman with desire. He had left his wives and sons in the care of Bhishma and Vidura.

Dhritarashtra became the sole ruler of Hastinapura and favoured his sons over his nephews. He gave them more power and privileges than the Pandavas. He also ignored Vidura's advice and listened to his son Duryodhana and his uncle Shakuni, who were evil and cunning.

They plotted to kill the Pandavas by burning them alive in a palace made of wax, which they had built for them as a gift. However, the Pandavas escaped with the help of Vidura, who had warned them beforehand. They went into hiding in the forest and disguised themselves as Brahmins, or priests.

They then attended the swayamvar of Draupadi, the princess of Panchala, who was renowned for her beauty and intelligence. She had set a difficult task for her suitors: they had to string a bow and shoot an arrow through a revolving fish eye, while looking at its reflection in a pool of water. Many kings and princes tried their luck, but failed.

Arjuna, however, succeeded in hitting the target and won Draupadi's hand. He then revealed his identity as a Pandava and took her to his mother Kunti. Kunti, without knowing that he had brought a bride, asked him to share whatever he had brought with his brothers. Arjuna obeyed her and told her that he had brought Draupadi.

Kunti was shocked and regretted her words. She did not want to break her son's promise or insult Draupadi by taking her back. She also did not want to create any discord among her sons or offend Draupadi's father Drupada, who was a powerful king and an ally.

She then consulted with Vyasa, who had come to visit them. Vyasa said that it was all part of a divine plan and that Draupadi was destined to be the wife of all five Pandavas. He said that she was an incarnation of Lakshmi, the goddess of wealth and fortune, who had chosen them as her husbands. He also said that they would be blessed with great fame and glory because of her.

Kunti then accepted Vyasa's words and agreed to let Draupadi marry all five Pandavas. Draupadi also agreed to this arrangement out of respect for Kunti and love for Arjuna. She became the common wife of all five Pandavas.

Dhritarashtra heard about this and was furious. He considered it an insult to his sons and an affront to his authority. He also feared that the Pandavas would become more powerful and popular than the Kauravas because of Draupadi.

He decided to pacify them by giving them half of his kingdom as their share. He gave them a barren land called Khandava-prastha, which was infested with snakes and demons. He hoped that they would perish there or lose their morale.

However, the Pandavas turned their misfortune into fortune with the help of Krishna, who was their cousin and friend. He was also an incarnation of Vishnu, the supreme god, who had come to earth to restore dharma, or righteousness.

Krishna helped them clear the forest of Khandava-prastha by setting it on fire with his discus Sudarshana. He also helped them build a magnificent city.

Later, Bhishma was called Bhishma-pitamaha (or the grandfather), and helped the kauravas in the mahabharata since he belonged to their kingdom.

Bhishma was put to the death bed in the war of Kurukshetra, by Arjuna; and Bhishma had set his journey to the heavens.

"Kumbhakarna: A Sleeping Giant's Rise and Fall"

<u>Birth</u>

Long ago, there lived a sage named Vishrava, who was the son of Pulastya, one of the mind-born sons of Brahma, the creator god. Vishrava had two wives: one was Devavarnini, a pious and noble woman, who gave birth to a son named Kubera, the lord of wealth and treasures; the other was Kaikesi, a wicked and ambitious woman, who belonged to the race of rakshasas, or demons. Kaikesi gave birth to four children: three sons named Ravana, Kumbhakarna, and Vibhishana; and a daughter named Surpanakha.

Ravana was the eldest son and the most powerful among them. He had ten heads and twenty arms, which symbolised his immense knowledge and strength. He was also a great devotee of Shiva, the destroyer god, and had received many boons from him. He was ambitious and arrogant, and wanted to conquer the three worlds: heaven, earth, and underworld.

Kumbhakarna was the second son and the most gigantic among them. He had a huge body and a huge appetite. He could eat anything and everything in his sight. He was also a great warrior and a master of many weapons. He was loyal and fearless, and fought to defend his brother and land out of obligation and affection.

Vibhishana was the third son and the most virtuous among them. He had a calm and gentle demeanour. He was also a great scholar and a follower of dharma, or righteousness. He was wise and compassionate, and tried to advise his brother to follow the path of truth and justice.

Shurpanakha was the only daughter and the most cunning among them. She had a beautiful face but an ugly heart. She was also a great sorceress and could change her form at will. She was greedy and lustful, and sought to seduce any man who caught her fancy.

The four siblings grew up together in Lanka, the island kingdom ruled by their father Vishrava. They learned various arts and sciences from their father and other teachers. They also performed many penances and sacrifices to please various gods and goddesses.

One day, Ravana decided to overthrow his half-brother Kubera from his throne in Alaka, the city of jewels located in Mount Kailasa, the abode of Shiva. He gathered a huge army of rakshasas and attacked Alaka with his brothers Kumbhakarna and Vibhishana by his side. Kubera could not withstand Ravana's might and fled from his kingdom with his followers. Ravana then occupied Lanka and seized Kubera's wealth and treasures, including his flying chariot Pushpaka Vimana.

Ravana then returned to Lanka with his brothers and celebrated his victory. He declared himself as the king of Lanka and appointed Kumbhakarna as his commander-in-chief and Vibhishana as his chief minister. He also made Shurpanakha as his favourite sister.

Ravana then embarked on a series of conquests to expand his empire. He defeated many kings and rulers of different lands and made them pay tribute to him. He also challenged many gods and sages in battles and defeated them with his boons from Shiva.

He became so powerful that he even dared to attack Indra, the king of gods, in heaven. He fought with Indra for a long time but could not defeat him because Indra had a weapon called Vajra, or thunderbolt, which was made from the bones of sage Dadhichi. Ravana then decided to use another strategy: he kidnapped Indra's wife Sachi Devi along with other celestial nymphs from heaven.

He brought them to Lanka in his Pushpaka Vimana and locked them in his palace. He then tried to force Sachi Devi to become his wife, but she resisted him and prayed to her husband for help.

Indra was furious and ashamed when he learned about Ravana's act. He gathered all the gods and prepared to wage a war against Ravana. He also sought the help of Vishnu, the preserver god, who was the supreme lord of all.

Vishnu agreed to help Indra and the gods. He said that he would incarnate as a human being on earth and destroy Ravana and his rakshasa army. He said that he would be born as the son of Dasharatha, the king of Ayodhya, and his wife Kaushalya. He said that his name would be Rama, and he would be the embodiment of dharma.

He also said that he would be accompanied by his consort Lakshmi, who would be born as the daughter of Janaka, the king of Mithila, and his wife Sunaina. She would be named Sita, and she would be the epitome of beauty and virtue.

He also said that he would be assisted by his brothers, friends, and allies, who would be incarnations of various gods and sages. He said that they would help him in his mission to restore peace and harmony in the world.

He then asked Indra to wait for his arrival on earth and assured him that he would rescue Sachi Devi and the other nymphs from Ravana's clutches.

Indra agreed to Vishnu's plan and decided to postpone his attack on Lanka. He also asked Sachi Devi and the other nymphs to endure their captivity for some time and have faith in Vishnu's promise.

Meanwhile, Ravana continued to rule over Lanka with pride and arrogance. He ignored Vibhishana's advice to release Sachi Devi and the other nymphs and return them to Indra. He also ignored Kumbhakarna's warning to beware of Vishnu's incarnation as Rama. He thought that he was invincible and no one could challenge him.

He was wrong.

Curse

One day, Ravana decided to perform a great penance to please Brahma, the creator god, and obtain more boons from him. He went to a secluded place and started to meditate on Brahma's name. He also cut off his heads one by one and offered them as a sacrifice to Brahma. He did this for a thousand years, until he had only one head left.

Brahma was impressed by Ravana's devotion and appeared before him. He asked him to stop his penance and ask for any boon he desired. Ravana asked for two boons: one, that he would be immortal and invulnerable to any weapon or being; and two, that he would be the supreme lord of the three worlds and no one could oppose him.

Brahma said that he could not grant him the first boon, as it was against the law of nature and karma. He said that every being had to die sooner or later, according to their actions and destiny. He also said that Ravana had already received enough boons from Shiva and other gods, which made him almost invincible.

He then asked him to modify his first book and choose another one. Ravana thought for a while and then asked for another boon: that he would be immune to death by any god, demon, human, animal, bird, or reptile. He thought that he had covered all the possible sources of danger and left no loophole.

Brahma agreed to grant him this boon, but warned him that he had overlooked some beings that could still harm him. He said that he had not mentioned monkeys, bears, and other forest creatures, who were considered as insignificant and harmless by Ravana. He also said that he had not mentioned women, who were considered as weak and inferior by Ravana.

He then granted him his second boon as well, but cautioned him that his arrogance and greed would lead to his downfall. He then disappeared.

Ravana was overjoyed by his boons and felt more confident and powerful than ever. He returned to Lanka with his brothers Kumbhakarna and Vibhishana by his side. He announced his boons to his people and declared himself as the immortal and invincible king of the three worlds.

He then resumed his conquests and oppressions with more vigour and cruelty. He attacked and plundered many kingdoms and realms. He also kidnapped and violated many women from different lands and races.

He became so notorious that he earned the name of Dashanan, or "the ten-headed one", which signified his evil nature and deeds.

Meanwhile, Kumbhakarna also decided to perform a penance to please Brahma and obtain some boons from him. He went to a secluded place and started to meditate on Brahma's name. He also performed many austerities and sacrifices for a thousand years.

Brahma was pleased by Kumbhakarna's devotion and appeared before him. He asked him to stop his penance and ask for any boon he desired. Kumbhakarna was about to ask for a boon, but before he could speak, he was interrupted by a voice.

The voice belonged to Saraswati, the goddess of learning and speech, who was also the consort of Brahma. She had been instructed by Vishnu to interfere with Kumbhakarna's boon, as part of his plan to defeat Ravana in the future.

She entered Kumbhakarna's mouth and twisted his tongue, so that he could not speak clearly. She made him say "Nidrasana", which means "sleeping seat", instead of "Indrasana", which means "throne of Indra".

Brahma heard this and was surprised. He asked Kumbhakarna if he really wanted a sleeping seat as his boon. Kumbhakarna realised his mistake and tried to correct himself, but it was too late.

Brahma said that he had already granted him his boon and could not take it back. He said that Kumbhakarna would sleep for six months at a stretch and wake up for only one day in a year. He said that this would be his fate for eternity.

Kumbhakarna was shocked and dismayed by this curse. He begged Brahma to revoke it or modify it somehow. Brahma said that he could not do anything about it now, but he could give him another boon: that he would be able to choose when he wanted to sleep or wake up.

He accepted this boon reluctantly and returned to Lanka with his brother Vibhishana by his side. He told Ravana about his curse and his boon. Ravana was saddened by his brother's fate and tried to console him. He said that he would always protect him and wake him up whenever he needed him.

He then asked him to sleep in a special chamber in his palace, which was large enough to accommodate his huge body. He also arranged for a large amount of food and drink to be kept near him, so that he could eat and drink as much as he wanted when he woke up.

Kumbhakarna thanked his brother for his kindness and affection. He then went to his chamber and lay down on his sleeping seat. He closed his eyes and fell asleep.

He slept for six months at a stretch and woke up for only one day in a year. He spent that day eating, drinking, and talking with his brothers and sister. He also asked them about the happenings in the world and gave them his advice and opinion.

He was unaware of the events that were unfolding on earth, which would soon change his life and destiny.

War

On earth, Rama grew up as the eldest son of Dasharatha and Kaushalya. He was handsome, brave, and righteous. He was also an expert archer and a master of many weapons. He was loved by his father, his brothers, his friends, and his people.

He had three brothers: Bharata, the son of Dasharatha and Kaikeyi; and Lakshmana and Shatrughna, the sons of Dasharatha and Sumitra. They were all devoted to Rama and followed him in his adventures.

He also had a friend and mentor: Vishwamitra, a sage and a king, who had taught him many secrets of the Vedas, the scriptures, and the mantras, the sacred chants. He had also given him many divine weapons and blessings.

He also had a wife: Sita, the daughter of Janaka and Sunaina. She was beautiful, virtuous, and faithful. She was also an incarnation of Lakshmi, the goddess of wealth and fortune. She had chosen Rama as her husband in her swayamvara, where she had set a difficult task for her suitors: they had to lift and string a bow that belonged to Shiva, which was so heavy that no one could even move it. Rama had not only lifted and strung the bow, but also broke it in half with his strength.

Rama was happy and content with his life in Ayodhya, the capital of his father's kingdom. He was also ready to become the king, as Dasharatha had decided to retire and crown him as his successor.

However, fate had other plans for him.

On the eve of his coronation, Dasharatha was reminded of a promise he had made to Kaikeyi long ago. He had promised her two boons for saving his life in a battle. She had not asked for them until then, but now she decided to use them for her own benefit.

She asked Dasharatha to banish Rama to the forest for fourteen years and make Bharata the king instead. She did this because she wanted her son to rule over Ayodhya and she feared that Rama would overshadow him.

Dasharatha was shocked and heartbroken by Kaikeyi's demand. He tried to dissuade her and persuade her to change her mind, but she was adamant and cruel. She threatened to kill herself if he did not fulfil her boons.

Dasharatha had no choice but to agree to her boons. He called Rama to his chamber and told him about his decision. He asked him to leave Ayodhya and live in exile for fourteen years.

Rama was surprised and saddened by his father's decision. He did not understand why he had to suffer such a fate for no fault of his own. However, he did not question or disobey his father's command. He accepted it as his duty and destiny.

He decided to leave Ayodhya with Sita and Lakshmana by his side. They were both loyal and loving to him and refused to stay behind. They said that they would share his joys and sorrows in the forest.

They then prepared to leave Ayodhya with their belongings and weapons. They bid farewell to their father, their brothers, their friends, and their people. They also sought the blessings of their elders and teachers.

They then boarded a chariot driven by Sumantra, Dasharatha's charioteer, who took them to the outskirts of Ayodhya. There they met Guha, the king of the Nishadas, who was a friend of Rama. He offered them food and shelter for the night.

The next day, they crossed the river Ganga on a boat provided by Guha. They then met Bharadwaja, a sage who lived in an ashram near Prayaga. He welcomed them warmly and offered them hospitality for some time.

They then moved further southwards towards Dandaka forest, where they planned to spend their exile period. They met many sages and ascetics on their way, who praised them for their courage and virtue..

They also faced many dangers and difficulties on their way, such as wild animals, harsh weather, and hostile rakshasas. They fought with many demons and monsters who tried to harm them or obstruct their path. They also helped many sages and hermits who were troubled by the rakshasas.

They finally reached a place called Panchavati, where they decided to settle down for some time. They built a hut of leaves and branches and lived there peacefully. They spent their days worshipping the gods, serving the sages, and enjoying the beauty of nature.

Meanwhile, in Lanka, Ravana was unaware of Rama's existence and whereabouts. He was busy enjoying his pleasures and luxuries with his wives and concubines. He was also proud of his boons and powers and thought that no one could challenge him.

He was wrong.

One day, he received a visit from his sister Shurpanakha, who had gone to Dandaka forest for some reason. She told him about Rama and Sita and how she had fallen in love with Rama. She also told him how Rama had rejected her advances and how Lakshmana had cut off her nose and ears as a punishment.

She then praised Sita's beauty and charm and said that she was the most suitable woman for Ravana. She urged him to kidnap Sita and make her his wife. She said that this would be a great revenge on Rama and Lakshmana for insulting her.

Ravana was intrigued by Shurpanakha's words and asked her to describe Sita in detail. She did so and said that Sita was like a goddess on earth. She said that she had fair skin, long hair, lotus eyes, rosy lips, slender waist, round hips, and graceful limbs. She said that she wore a yellow silk saree, a red blouse, a golden necklace, earrings, bangles, anklets, and a crown of flowers. She said that she smelled like jasmine and sandalwood.

Ravana was enchanted by Shurpanakha's description and felt a surge of lust in his heart. He decided to kidnap Sita and make her his wife. He thanked Shurpanakha for her information and asked her to wait for his return.

He then summoned Maricha, a rakshasa who was his uncle and friend. He told him about his plan to kidnap Sita and asked him to help him. He said that he wanted Maricha to disguise himself as a golden deer and lure Sita away from Rama. He said that he would then take advantage of the situation and abduct Sita in his Pushpaka Vimana.

Maricha was scared and reluctant to help Ravana. He knew about Rama's prowess and power and warned Ravana not to mess with him. He said that Rama was not an ordinary human being but an incarnation of Vishnu himself. He said that Ravana would only invite his own doom by kidnapping Sita.

He also reminded Ravana of his previous encounter with Rama in Rajasthan, where he had gone to harass the sages along with Khara, Dushana, Trishira, and fourteen thousand other rakshasas. He said that Rama had single-handedly killed all of them with his arrows, except for him, whom he had spared out of mercy.

He begged Ravana to drop his plan and leave Sita alone. He said that she was not worth risking his life and kingdom for.

And then, all the story that was mentioned in chapter one was bound to happen, and Kumbhakarna had to die before Ravana.

Savitri: A Faithful Wife's Resolve and Success

<u>Choice</u>

Long ago, there lived a king named Ashvapati, who ruled over the kingdom of Madra. He was a wise and just ruler, loved by his people and respected by his enemies. He was also a great devotee of Savitri, the goddess of the sun, who granted long life to humans and immortality to the gods. He performed many sacrifices and penances in her honour, hoping to get a son from her.

However, he remained childless for many years. He prayed to Savitri with more fervour and intensity, asking her to bless him with a child. Finally, the goddess was pleased with his devotion and appeared before him. She asked him to choose a boon from her.

Ashvapati asked for a son who would continue his lineage and inherit his throne. The goddess said that she could not grant him that boon, as it was against his destiny. She said that he would only have a daughter from her, who would be named after her.

Ashvapati accepted the goddess's will and thanked her for her boon. He then returned to his palace and told his wife about his encounter with Savitri.

Soon, his wife became pregnant and gave birth to a beautiful girl. She was named Savitri by her father, in honour of the goddess. She grew up to be a lovely and virtuous woman, endowed with divine qualities. She was also well-versed in various arts and sciences, and had a keen interest in spirituality.

She was so charming and graceful that no man dared to ask for her hand in marriage. Her father was worried about her future and decided to let her choose her own husband. He asked her to travel around the country with some ministers and find a suitable match for herself.

Savitri agreed to her father's wish and set out on her journey in a golden chariot. She visited many kingdoms and met many princes and nobles, but none of them appealed to her heart.

One day, she reached a forest where she saw a young man cutting wood with an axe. He was handsome and strong, with bright eyes and curly hair. He wore simple clothes and had a cheerful smile on his face.

Savitri felt drawn to him and asked him who he was and where he lived. He said that he was Satyavan, the son of Dyumatsena, the former king of Shalva. He said that his father had lost his sight and his kingdom due to a curse from an enemy. He said that he now lived in exile in the forest with his parents, leading a life of hardship and poverty.

Savitri was moved by his story and admired his courage and loyalty. She felt that he was the one she had been looking for all along. She decided to marry him and make him happy.

She then returned to her father's palace and told him about her choice. Her father was surprised and saddened by her decision. He said that Satyavan was not worthy of her, as he was poor and powerless. He also said that he had consulted the sage Narada, who had told him that Satyavan was doomed to die within a year.

He pleaded with Savitri to change her mind and choose another husband who could give her a better life. He said that he did not want to lose his only daughter so soon.

She said that she had given her heart to Satyavan and could not love anyone else. She said that she was ready to face any fate with him, even death. She said that she had faith in Savitri, the goddess of the sun, who would protect her and her husband.

She then asked her father to respect her choice and give her his blessing. She said that she would not marry Satyavan without his consent and approval.

Ashvapati was touched by Savitri's sincerity and devotion. He realised that she was a true daughter of Savitri, the goddess, and had inherited her qualities. He also realised that he could not force her to do something against her will.

He decided to honour Savitri's wish and agreed to let her marry Satyavan. He gave her his blessing and asked her to be happy and faithful to her husband.

He then arranged for Savitri's wedding with Satyavan in a simple and solemn ceremony. He invited the sage Narada and other sages and priests to officiate the marriage. He also invited Satyavan's parents, Dyumatsena and his wife, who were overjoyed by their son's marriage.

Savitri and Satyavan exchanged garlands and vows in front of the sacred fire. They then circumambulated the fire seven times, signifying their seven promises to each other. They then touched the feet of their elders and teachers and sought their blessings.

They then left Ayodhya with their belongings and weapons. They boarded a chariot driven by Sumantra, Ashvapati's charioteer, who took them to the forest where Satyavan lived with his parents.

They reached the forest and met Dyumatsena and his wife, who welcomed them warmly. They offered them food and shelter in their hut of leaves and branches. They also gave them their love and affection.

Savitri and Satyavan settled down in the forest and lived there happily. They spent their days serving their parents-in-law, worshipping the gods, serving the sages, and enjoying the beauty of nature.

They also loved each other deeply and sincerely. They shared their joys and sorrows, hopes and fears, dreams and desires. They were like two bodies with one soul.

Love

Savitri and Satyavan lived in the forest for a year, blissfully unaware of the impending doom. They loved each other more and more with each passing day. They were like the sun and the moon, the fire and the wind, the earth and the sky.

They also earned the respect and admiration of everyone who met them. They were kind and generous to the poor and needy, humble and courteous to the elders and sages, brave and righteous to the enemies and oppressors.

They were also blessed by many gods and goddesses, who were pleased by their devotion and virtue. They gave them many gifts and boons, such as health, wealth, happiness, wisdom, and power.

However, there was one god who was not happy with them. He was Yama, the god of death, who had marked Satyavan's life span with his noose. He knew that Satyavan's time was up and he had to take him away from Savitri.

He decided to do his duty on the day when Satyavan completed his one year of marriage with Savitri. He waited for that day with patience and determination.

Meanwhile, Savitri had a premonition of something bad happening to her husband. She felt a sense of fear and anxiety in her heart. She did not know what it was or why it was happening, but she decided to be more careful and attentive to her husband.

She also performed a special penance called Savitri Vrata, or Savitri's vow, in honour of Savitri, the goddess of the sun. She fasted for three days and three nights, without eating or drinking anything. She prayed to Savitri for her husband's long life and well-being.

She also asked her parents-in-law for their permission to accompany Satyavan wherever he went in the forest. They agreed to her request and blessed her for her love and loyalty.

She then followed Satyavan everywhere he went in the forest. She helped him in cutting wood, collecting fruits, fetching water, making fire, and doing other chores. She also sang songs, told stories, cracked jokes, and played games with him. She tried to make him happy and cheerful.

Satyavan was touched by Savitri's affection and care. He thanked her for being his wife and friend. He said that he was lucky to have her in his life. He said that he could not ask for anything more from the gods.

Death

The day came when Satyavan completed his one year of marriage with Savitri. It was a bright and sunny day, with a clear blue sky and a gentle breeze. Savitri and Satyavan woke up early and performed their morning prayers. They then ate some fruits and drank some water.

They then decided to go to the forest to cut some wood for their hut. Savitri insisted on accompanying Satyavan, as she always did. Satyavan agreed and took his axe and basket with him. Savitri also took her basket and followed him.

They reached a spot in the forest where there were many trees and plants. Satyavan chose a big and sturdy tree and started to chop it with his axe. Savitri helped him by collecting the fallen branches and putting them in her basket.

They worked for some time, chatting and laughing with each other. They did not notice that someone was watching them from a distance. He was Yama, the god of death, who had come to take Satyavan's life away.

He waited for the right moment to strike. He saw that Satyavan was sweating and panting from his exertion. He also saw that Savitri was busy in her work and not paying attention to her husband.

He then threw his noose around Satyavan's neck and pulled it tight. He severed Satyavan's soul from his body and captured it in his noose.

Satyavan felt a sudden pain in his chest and dropped his axe. He staggered towards Savitri and fell into her arms. He looked at her with love and said, "Savitri, I feel faint and weak. I think I am dying. Please take care of my parents and yourself. I love you."

He then closed his eyes and breathed his last.

Savitri was shocked and horrified by what had happened. She felt her husband's body go limp and cold in her arms. She saw his face turn pale and lifeless. She heard his voice fade away in her ears.

She could not believe that he was gone. She cried out loud, "Satyavan, Satyavan, wake up! Don't leave me alone! You are my life, my soul, my everything! How can I live without you?"

She then saw Yama standing near them, holding his noose with Satyavan's soul in it. She recognized him as the god of death and realised that he had taken her husband away from her.

She was angry and defiant. She said to Yama, "How dare you take my husband away from me? He is mine and only mine! You have no right to separate us! Give him back to me or face my wrath!"

Yama said to Savitri, "Do not be foolish, Savitri. Your husband's time on earth is over. He has to come with me to the abode of the dead, where he will face the consequences of his actions. You cannot stop me or change his fate."

He then turned around and started to walk away with Satyavan's soul in his noose.

Savitri did not give up or lose hope. She decided to follow Yama and persuade him to return her husband to her. She left Satyavan's body on the ground and ran after Yama.

She said to Yama, "Wait, Yama! You cannot go without me! I am Satyavan's wife and I have a right to be with him wherever he goes! I will not let you take him away from me!"

Yama said to Savitri, "Stop following me, Savitri. You are wasting your time and energy. You cannot come with me to the abode of the dead, as you are still alive. You have to stay on earth and perform your duties as a widow."

Savitri said to Yama, "I do not care about my duties or my life on earth. I only care about my husband and my love for him. I will not leave him alone in your hands. I will follow you till the end of the world!"

Yama said to Savitri, "You are stubborn and foolish, Savitri. You do not know what you are asking for or what you are getting into. You do not know the horrors

You do not know the horrors and torments that await you in the abode of the dead. You do not know the pain and suffering that you will endure for your husband's sake. You do not know the price that you will pay for your love."

Savitri said to Yama, "I do not fear any horror or torment, any pain or suffering, any price or sacrifice. I only fear losing my husband and living without him. I only fear being separated from him and forgetting him. I only fear dishonouring my love and breaking my vow."

Yama said to Savitri, "You are brave and faithful, Savitri. I admire your courage and devotion. But you are also naive and ignorant, Savitri. You do not understand the laws of nature and karma, Savitri. You do not respect the authority of death and destiny, Savitri."

Savitri said to Yama, "You are wise and powerful, Yama. I respect your knowledge and authority. But you are also cold and cruel, Yama. You do not understand the power of love and faith, Yama. You do not appreciate the value of life and freedom, Yama."

Yama said to Savitri, "You are clever and eloquent, Savitri. You have a sharp tongue and a quick wit. But you are also wasting your breath and time, Savitri. You cannot change my mind or heart, Savitri. You cannot win this argument or battle, Savitri."

Savitri said to Yama, "You are stubborn and arrogant, Yama. You have a closed mind and a hard heart. But you are also bound by your duty and rules, Yama. You have to follow your code and ethics, Yama. You have to listen to me and grant me a boon, Yama."

Yama said to Savitri, "What boon do you want from me, Savitri? What can I give you that will satisfy you, Savitri? What can I do for you that will make you stop following me, Savitri?"

Savitri said to Yama, "You can give me anything that is within your power and does not violate your duty, Yama. You can give me anything that is good and noble and does not harm anyone else, Yama. You can give me anything that will make me happy and grateful to you, Yama."

Yama said to Savitri, "Very well, Savitri. I will give you a boon of your choice, as long as it meets these conditions. But remember this: I will not give you back your husband's life or soul. That is beyond my power and against my duty."

Savitri said to Yama, "I understand, Yama. I will not ask for that boon from you. I will ask for something else that is within your power and does not violate your duty."

She then thought for a while and asked for her first boon: that her father-in-law Dyumatsena would regain his sight and his kingdom.

Yama said to Savitri, "That is an easy boon to grant, Savitri. Your father-in-law Dyumatsena will regain his sight and his kingdom as soon as you return to him. He will be happy and prosperous again."

He then granted her her first boon.

Savitri thanked him for her first boon and continued to follow him.

She then thought for a while and asked for her second boon: that her father Ashvapati would have many sons to continue his lineage.

Yama said to Savitri

Alright, here is the continuation of the story:

Yama said to Savitri, "That is also an easy boon to grant, Savitri. Your father Ashvapati will have many sons to continue his lineage. He will be happy and proud of his children."

He then granted her her second boon.

Savitri thanked him for her second boon and continued to follow him.

She then thought for a while and asked for her third boon: that she would have many children with Satyavan.

Yama said to Savitri, "That is a clever boon to ask, Savitri. You are trying to trick me into giving you back your husband's life. But you cannot fool me, Savitri. I will grant you your third boon, but only on one condition: that you will have children with Satyavan only if he is alive."

Savitri said to Yama, "I accept your condition, Yama. I know that you are bound by your duty and rules, Yama. But I also know that you are fair and just, Yama. You will not deny me my right as a wife and a mother, Yama."

She then smiled and said, "You have already granted me my third boon, Yama. You have already given me back my husband's life, Yama. For how can I have children with Satyavan if he is not alive?"

Yama was stunned and speechless by Savitri's words. He realised that she had outwitted him and won her husband's life back from him. He admired her intelligence and devotion. He also felt ashamed of his mistake and regretted his condition.

He then said to Savitri, "You are truly a remarkable woman, Savitri. You have defeated me with your wisdom and faith. You have earned your husband's life back from me. I cannot take him away from you now."

He then granted her her third boon without any condition.

Savitri thanked him for her third boon and bowed down to him.

She then asked him for one more favour: that he would forgive her for her audacity and boldness. She said that she did not mean to offend him or challenge him. She said that she only acted out of love and duty.

Yama said to Savitri, "You do not need to ask for my forgiveness, Savitri. You have not offended me or challenged me. You have only impressed me and inspired me. You have shown me the power of love and faith. You have taught me the value of life and freedom."

He then blessed her and said, "May you and your husband live long and happy lives together. May you have many children who will inherit your virtues and glory. May you be an example of a faithful wife and a successful woman for all times."

He then released Satyavan's soul from his noose and returned it to his body.

He then disappeared.

Life

Savitri was overjoyed to see her husband's soul return to his body. She hugged him and kissed him and thanked Yama for his boon. She then sprinkled some water on his face and rubbed his chest to revive him.

Satyavan slowly opened his eyes and saw Savitri's face. He smiled and said, "Savitri, you are here. I am so happy to see you. I had a strange dream. I saw Yama, the god of death, taking me away from you. I also saw you following him and arguing with him. I heard you asking for some boons from him. What was that all about?"

Savitri said, "It was not a dream, Satyavan. It was real. Yama had come to take your life away from me. But I followed him and persuaded him to give me back to me. He granted me four boons: that your father would regain his sight and his kingdom, that my father would have many sons, that we would have many children, and that you would live a long and happy life with me."

Satyavan was amazed and grateful by Savitri's words. He said, "You are truly a remarkable woman, Savitri. You have saved my life with your wisdom and faith. You have earned my love with your courage and devotion. You have made me the happiest man in the world."

He then hugged her and kissed her and thanked her for being his wife.

They then collected their wood and baskets and returned to their hut. They met Dyumatsena and his wife, who were waiting for them anxiously.

They were surprised and delighted to see that Dyumatsena had regained his sight and could see them clearly. They also heard a messenger from Shalva, who had come to inform them that the enemy king who had cursed Dyumatsena had died of a disease and that his people had invited Dyumatsena to return to his kingdom as their rightful king.

They were overjoyed by this news and decided to leave the forest and go back to Shalva. They also invited Savitri and Satyavan to come with them and live in their palace.

Savitri and Satyavan agreed to go with them, but they also wanted to visit Ayodhya and meet Savitri's parents. They said goodbye to their forest friends and boarded the chariot driven by Sumantra, who had come to take them back.

They reached Ayodhya and met Ashvapati and his wife, who were overjoyed to see them alive and well. They also learned that Ashvapati had been blessed with many sons by Savitri's boon.

They then celebrated Savitri's return and Satyavan's recovery with great joy and pomp. They also thanked Savitri, the goddess of the sun, for her grace and protection.

They then left Ayodhya with their parents-in-law and went to Shalva, where they were welcomed by the people as their king and queen.

They lived happily ever after in Shalva, ruling their kingdom with justice and compassion. They also had many children who inherited their virtues and glory.

They were an example of a faithful wife and a successful woman for all times.

Nala and Damayanti: A Loving Couple's Trial and Triumph

Choice

Long ago, there lived a king named Nala, who ruled over the kingdom of Nishadha. He was a handsome and brave ruler, skilled in archery and chariot-driving. He was also a righteous and generous king, loved by his people and respected by his allies. He had everything he wanted, except for one thing: a wife.

He had not found a woman who could match his beauty and virtue, who could be his companion and partner in life. He longed for someone who could understand him and love him for who he was.

Meanwhile, in another kingdom called Vidarbha, there lived a princess named Damayanti. She was the daughter of King Bhima and Queen Sudeshna. She was the most beautiful woman in the world, with fair skin, long hair, lotus eyes, rosy lips, slender waist, round hips, and graceful limbs. She was also a wise and virtuous woman, well-versed in various arts and sciences, and had a keen interest in spirituality.

She had many suitors who came from far and wide to seek her hand in marriage. But she had not found a man who could match her beauty and virtue, who could be her companion and partner in life. She longed for someone who could understand her and love her for who she was.

One day, Nala captured a swan in the forest. The swan pleaded for its life and promised to do him a favour in return. Nala agreed to spare the swan's life and asked what it could do for him. The swan said that it knew of a woman who was perfect for him: Damayanti.

The swan praised Damayanti's beauty and charm and said that she was the only one who could make him happy. Nala was intrigued by the swan's words and asked it to tell him more about Damayanti. The swan said that it would fly to Vidarbha and speak highly of Nala to Damayanti, persuading her to choose him as her husband.

Nala agreed to this plan and let the swan go.

The swan flew to Vidarbha and found Damayanti in her garden with her friends. It landed near her feet and caught her attention. It then spoke to her in human language and told her about Nala.

It praised Nala's beauty and courage and said that he was the only one who could make her happy. Damayanti was amazed by the swan's words and asked it to tell her more about Nala. The swan said that it would fly back to Nishadha and bring Nala to Vidarbha, so that she could see him for herself.

Damayanti agreed to this plan and waited for the swan's return.

The swan flew back to Nishadha and told Nala about Damayanti's interest in him. It urged him to go to Vidarbha with it and meet her in person. Nala agreed to this plan and followed the swan.

The swan took Nala to Vidarbha and showed him the way to Damayanti's garden. Nala entered the garden and saw Damayanti sitting with her friends. He was stunned by her beauty and grace. He felt a surge of love and admiration in his heart.

He approached her and bowed down to her. He introduced himself as Nala, the king of Nishadha, and said that he had come to see her on the swan's recommendation. He said that he had heard a lot about her from the swan and wanted to meet her in person.

Damayanti recognized him as the one whom the swan had praised to her. She was also stunned by his beauty and courage. She felt a surge of love and respect in her heart.

She welcomed him and asked him to sit with her. She introduced herself as Damayanti, the daughter of Bhima, the king of Vidarbha, and said that she had been waiting for him at the swan's suggestion. She said that she had heard a lot about him from the swan and wanted to see him for herself.

They then talked to each other for a long time, exchanging their views and feelings. They found that they had a lot in common and understood each other well. They felt a strong connection and attraction between them.

They then realised that they had fallen in love with each other and decided to marry each other. They exchanged their garlands and vows in front of the swan, who acted as their witness. They then hugged each other and kissed each other.

They then decided to inform their parents about their marriage and seek their approval. They left the garden with the swan and went to their respective palaces.

They met their parents and told them about their love and marriage. Their parents were surprised and happy by their choice. They agreed to their marriage and blessed them for their happiness.

They then arranged for their wedding in a grand and solemn ceremony. They invited many kings and princes, sages and priests, friends and relatives, to witness their marriage. They also invited the gods and goddesses, who were pleased by their love and virtue.

Nala and Damayanti exchanged garlands and vows in front of the sacred fire. They then circumambulated the fire seven times, signifying their seven promises to each other. They then touched the feet of their elders and teachers and sought their blessings.

They then left Vidarbha with their belongings and weapons. They boarded a chariot driven by Varshneya, Nala's charioteer, who took them to Nishadha.

They reached Nishadha and were welcomed by the people as their king and queen.

They lived happily ever after in Nishadha, ruling their kingdom with justice and compassion. They also had many children who inherited their virtues and glory.

They were an example of a loving couple who faced many trials and triumphed over them with their love and faith.

<u>Separation</u>

Nala and Damayanti lived in Nishadha for a year, blissfully unaware of the impending doom. They loved each other more and more with each passing day. They were like the sun and the moon, the fire and the wind, the earth and the sky.

They also earned the respect and admiration of everyone who met them. They were kind and generous to the poor and needy, humble and courteous to the elders and sages, brave and righteous to the enemies and oppressors.

They also received many gifts and boons from the gods and goddesses, who were pleased by their devotion and virtue. They gave them health, wealth, happiness, wisdom, and power.

However, there was one god who was not happy with them. He was Kali, the god of evil and misfortune, who had a grudge against Nala. He had wanted to marry Damayanti himself, but he had lost to Nala in her swayamvara. He had not forgotten or forgiven his defeat. He wanted to take revenge on Nala and ruin his life.

He decided to do his evil deed on the day when Nala completed his one year of marriage with Damayanti. He waited for that day with malice and cunning.

Meanwhile, Nala had a passion for gambling. He loved to play dice with his friends and ministers. He was also very good at it and rarely lost. He played for fun and sport, not for greed or pride.

He did not know that gambling was a dangerous game that could lead to his downfall. He did not know that Kali had a plan to use his weakness against him.

He was wrong.

The day came when Nala completed his one year of marriage with Damayanti. It was a bright and sunny day, with a clear blue sky and a gentle breeze. Nala and Damayanti woke up early and performed their morning prayers. They then ate some fruits and drank some water.

They then decided to go to the court and attend to their duties as king and queen. They left their palace with their belongings and weapons. They boarded a chariot driven by Varshneya, Nala's charioteer, who took them to the court.

They reached the court and were welcomed by their ministers and subjects. They sat on their thrones and listened to the reports and petitions of their people. They solved their problems and granted their requests with justice and compassion.

They then received a visit from Pushkara, Nala's brother, who had come from another kingdom. He greeted them warmly and congratulated them on their anniversary. He said that he had brought a gift for them: a set of golden dice.

Nala was pleased by his brother's gift and thanked him for it. He said that he loved to play dice and asked him if he wanted to play with him. Pushkara agreed and said that he would play with him for fun and sport.

Nala agreed and asked Damayanti to join them. Damayanti declined and said that she did not like to play dice. She said that it was a risky and addictive game that could lead to trouble and sorrow. She advised Nala to be careful and moderate in his gambling.

Nala said that he appreciated her concern, but he assured her that he knew his limits and would not gamble more than he could afford.

He said that he trusted his brother and would not cheat or be cheated by him. He said that he just wanted to have some fun and entertainment with him.

Damayanti agreed to let him play, but she also warned him to be alert and vigilant. She said that she would watch over him and support him.

Nala then went to the dice hall with Pushkara and sat down to play with him. They agreed on the stakes and rules of the game. They then started to roll the dice and place their bets.

Nala did not know that Pushkara was in league with Kali, who had entered his dice and manipulated them. He also did not know that Kali had entered his body and influenced his mind. He was unaware of the trap that was set for him.

He soon found out that he was losing every round of the game. He lost his money, his jewels, his clothes, his weapons, his chariot, his horses, his elephants, his palace, his kingdom, and everything else he owned.

He was shocked and bewildered by his bad luck. He could not understand how he could lose so much so fast. He could not believe that his brother could cheat him so cruelly.

He then realised that he had only one thing left to lose: his wife.

He looked at Damayanti, who was watching him with tears in her eyes. She was sad and scared by what had happened to him. She was also angry and disgusted by what Pushkara had done to him.

She then saw Pushkara looking at her with lust in his eyes. He said to Nala, "You have nothing left to bet, Nala. You have lost everything you had, Nala. You have only one thing left to offer me: your wife."

He then asked Nala to stake Damayanti in the next round of the game. He said that if Nala won, he would give him back everything he had lost. But if Nala lost, he would take Damayanti as his prize.

Nala was outraged and offended by Pushkara's demand. He said that he would never stake his wife in a game of dice. He said that she was his life, his soul, his everything. He said that she was not a thing to be gambled or won.

He then refused to play any more with Pushkara. He said that he had enough of his cheating and treachery. He said that he would rather die than lose his wife to him.

He then got up from his seat and walked away from the dice hall with Damayanti by his side.

Pushkara laughed and mocked him for being a coward and a loser. He said that he had won everything from him fair and square. He said that he was now the king of Nishadha and Damayanti was now his queen.

He then ordered his men to capture Nala and Damayanti and bring them to him.

Nala fought back with all his strength and courage

He fought back with all his strength and courage, but he was outnumbered and overpowered by Pushkara's men. They seized him and Damayanti and dragged them to Pushkara.

Pushkara looked at them with contempt and said, "You are no longer the king and queen of Nishadha, Nala and Damayanti. You are now my slaves and prisoners. You will do as I say and serve me as I please. You will have no rights or dignity or freedom."

He then ordered his men to strip them of their clothes and jewels and throw them in a dungeon. He said that he would decide their fate later.

Nala and Damayanti were humiliated and tortured by Pushkara's men. They were beaten and starved and insulted. They were separated from each other and locked in different cells.

They suffered a lot, but they did not lose hope or faith. They prayed to the gods for their help and protection. They also remembered their love for each other and drew strength from it.

They decided to escape from Pushkara's clutches and reunite with each other. They waited for an opportunity to do so.

They did not know that the gods had heard their prayers and were planning to help them. They did not know that Kali's curse was about to end and Nala's luck was about to change.

One night, Nala managed to break free from his cell. He found a sword and a cloak in the guard's room. He put on the cloak and took the sword. He then went to Damayanti's cell and unlocked it. He was overjoyed to see her and hugged her tightly. He said, "My dear Damayanti, I have come to rescue you. Let us escape from this hell and find our way back to our kingdom."

Damayanti was also overjoyed to see him and hugged him back. She said, "My dear Nala, I have been waiting for this moment. Let us flee from this tyrant and seek justice for our wrongs."

They quickly left the dungeon and headed towards the gate. They saw that there were many guards and soldiers patrolling the palace. They decided to wait until they were asleep or distracted.

They hid behind a wall and waited for an hour. They saw that some of the guards were drinking and playing dice. They saw that some of the soldiers were sleeping or chatting. They saw that there was a gap in the security near the gate.

They seized the opportunity and ran towards the gate. They killed or wounded anyone who tried to stop them. They reached the gate and opened it.

They saw that there was a horse tied to a post outside the gate. They recognized it as Nala's horse, which he had lost in the game of dice. They were surprised and happy to see it.

They untied the horse and mounted it. They rode away from Pushkara's palace as fast as they could.

They did not know that this was a sign of their fortune turning in their favour. They did not know that Kali's curse had ended and Nala's luck had returned.

They did not know that the gods had helped them in their escape. They did not know that Indra, the king of gods, had sent his messenger Matali to bring Nala's horse to them.

They did not know that they were about to meet an old friend who would help them in their quest.

They did not know that they were about to face a new challenge that would test their love and faith.

They did not know that they were about to witness a miracle that would change their lives forever.

They only knew that they loved each other and trusted each other.

They only knew that they had escaped from Pushkara's clutches and reunited with each other.

They only knew that they had hope for a better future.

Okay, I will continue with the fourth part of the story. Here it is:

Nala and Damayanti rode for a long time, until they reached a dense forest. They decided to rest there for a while. They dismounted from the horse and tied it to a tree. They found a shady spot under a banyan tree and sat down.

They looked at each other and smiled. They felt relieved and happy to be together again. They thanked the gods for their mercy and grace.

They also felt hungry and thirsty. They had not eaten or drunk anything since they escaped from Pushkara's palace. They decided to look for some food and water in the forest.

They agreed to go in different directions and meet at the same spot after an hour. They took their sword and cloak with them and left.

Nala went towards the east, while Damayanti went towards the west. They searched for fruits, berries, roots, or herbs that they could eat or drink. They also looked for streams, ponds, or wells that they could quench their thirst.

Nala found a mango tree that was laden with ripe fruits. He plucked some of them and ate them. He felt refreshed and satisfied. He also found a spring that was gushing with clear water. He drank from it and filled his cloak with some water. He thought of Damayanti and hoped that she had also found something to eat and drink.

He decided to return to the banyan tree and wait for her. He took his sword and cloak with him and walked back.

Damayanti found a jackfruit tree that was full of large fruits. She cut one of them with her sword and ate some of its flesh. She felt nourished and energised. She also found a lake that was sparkling with blue water. She drank from it and washed her face and hands. She thought of Nala and wished that he had also found something to eat and drink.

She decided to return to the banyan tree and meet him. She took her sword and cloak with her and walked back.

As they were walking back, they did not know that they were being watched by someone who had evil intentions towards them.

They did not know that it was Kali, the demon who had cursed Nala and caused all his troubles.

They did not know that Kali was furious that Nala had escaped from his curse and regained his luck.

They did not know that Kali was determined to ruin their happiness and separate them again.

They did not know that Kali had a plan to deceive them and create a misunderstanding between them.

They did not know that Kali had disguised himself as Nala and was waiting for Damayanti near the banyan tree.

Damayanti reached the banyan tree and saw Nala waiting for her. She ran towards him and hugged him. She said, "My dear Nala, I have found some food and water for us. Let us eat and drink and then resume our journey."

Nala hugged her back and said, "My dear Damayanti, I have also found some food and water for us. Let us eat and drink and then resume our journey."

They sat down under the tree and shared their food and water. They ate and drank with joy and gratitude.

They did not know that the Nala who was with Damayanti was not the real Nala, but Kali in disguise.

They did not know that Kali had used his magic to make himself look like Nala, sound like Nala, and smell like Nala.

They did not know that Kali had a wicked plan to seduce Damayanti and make her betray Nala.

They did not know that Kali had waited for Damayanti to return, while the real Nala was still on his way back.

They did not know that Kali had prepared a trap for them, which would soon be sprung.

Nala reached the banyan tree and saw Damayanti sitting with another Nala. He was shocked and confused. He said, "Who are you? How can there be two of me? What are you doing with my wife?"

Damayanti heard his voice and looked up. She saw another Nala standing before her. She was also shocked and confused. She said, "Who are you? How can there be two of you? What are you doing here?"

Kali saw that his plan had worked. He smiled wickedly and said, "I am the real Nala, and this is an impostor who has deceived you. He is a demon who has taken my form to lure you away from me. He is your enemy and mine."

The real Nala said, "No, he is lying. I am the real Nala, and he is the demon who has cursed me and caused all my troubles. He is Kali, the lord of evil. He is your enemy and mine."

Damayanti looked at both of them and could not tell them apart. They both looked exactly like Nala, spoke exactly like Nala, and acted exactly like Nala.

She did not know whom to believe or trust.

She did not know how to find out the truth.

She did not know what to do.

She decided to use her intelligence and intuition to solve the mystery.

She said, "If you are both Nala, then you must both love me. Tell me, how much do you love me?"

Kali said, "I love you more than anything in the world. I love you more than life itself. I love you more than myself."

Nala said, "I love you as much as you love me. I love you as much as I love myself. I love you as much as God loves us."

Damayanti heard their answers and realised who was who.

She knew that Kali was lying and boasting, while Nala was telling the truth and being humble.

She knew that Kali loved only himself, while Nala loved her as his equal.

She knew that Kali wanted to possess her, while Nala wanted to share with her.

She knew that Kali was the demon, while Nala was her husband.

She said, "You are not Nala, you are Kali. You are a liar and a cheat. You have tried to trick me and harm me. You have failed miserably. You have no place in my heart or in my life."

She then turned to the real Nala and said, "You are my Nala, my husband and my friend. You are a hero and a king. You have faced many difficulties and dangers with courage and faith. You have won my respect and admiration. You have all my love and loyalty."

She then embraced him and kissed him.

Nala embraced her back and kissed her.

They were happy and relieved to have passed the test.

They did not know that the gods had witnessed their ordeal and were pleased with their outcome.

They did not know that Indra had sent his messenger Matali to help them in their quest.

They did not know that Matali had arrived at that moment with a chariot drawn by four white horses.

They did not know that Matali had a message for them from Indra.

They did not know that Indra had invited them to his heaven for a visit.

They did not know that Indra had a gift for them that would restore their kingdom and glory.

They only knew that they loved each other and trusted each other.

They only knew that they had escaped from Pushkara's clutches and reunited with each other.

They only knew that they had hope for a better future.

Abhimanyu: A Brave Prince's Valor and Martyrdom

A long time ago, in ancient India, there was a great war between two groups of cousins: the Pandavas and the Kauravas. The Pandavas were five noble brothers who were the rightful heirs to the throne of Hastinapura, the capital of the Kuru kingdom. The Kauravas were one hundred wicked brothers who had usurped the throne by cheating and plotting against the Pandavas. The war was called the Kurukshetra War, and it lasted for eighteen days. It was a war that involved many kings, warriors, sages, and gods. It was a war that decided the fate of the world.

Among the heroes of this war was a young prince named Abhimanyu. He was the son of Arjuna, the third and most famous of the Pandava brothers, and Subhadra, the sister of Lord Krishna, the supreme god who was also the friend and guide of the Pandavas. Abhimanyu was born with a divine destiny. He was the reincarnation of Varchas, the son of Chandra Dev, the moon god. Chandra Dev had agreed to send his son to earth for a short time to help the Pandavas in their righteous cause. He had also asked that his son should return to him after sixteen years.

Abhimanyu grew up to be a handsome, brave, and talented prince. He learned many skills from his father Arjuna, who was the best archer in the world. He also learned from his uncle Krishna, who taught him many secrets of warfare and spirituality. He also learned from his grandfather Indra, who gave him celestial weapons and armour. Abhimanyu was also loved by his mother Subhadra, who cared for him with affection and devotion.

Abhimanyu married Uttara, the daughter of King Virata of Matsya kingdom. He had met her when he had accompanied his father Arjuna in disguise to live in Virata's palace for one year. This was part of a condition that the Pandavas had to fulfil after they had lost their kingdom in a game of dice to the Kauravas. They had to spend twelve years in exile in the forest, followed by one year in hiding among people without being recognized. If they were discovered during this year, they had to repeat the whole process again.

Abhimanyu and Uttara fell in love with each other and got married with the blessings of their parents and elders. They were very happy together and looked forward to a bright future.

However, their happiness was short-lived. Soon after their marriage, the Kurukshetra War broke out between the Pandavas and the Kauravas. Abhimanyu joined his father Arjuna and his uncles Yudhishthira, Bhima,

Nakula, and Sahadeva in fighting for their rightful kingdom against their evil cousins Duryodhana, Dushasana, Karna, and others. Abhimanyu proved himself to be a valiant warrior who fought with courage and skill. He defeated many enemies and earned fame and respect.

On the thirteenth day of the war, however, he faced his greatest challenge and tragedy. The Kaurava army formed a deadly formation called Chakravyuha or Padmavyuha. This was a circular or lotus-shaped formation that had many layers or rings of soldiers surrounding a central core. It was very difficult to enter this formation and even more difficult to exit from it. Only a few warriors knew how to break this formation.

One of them was Arjuna, who had learned it from his teacher Dronacharya, who was now fighting on the side of the Kauravas. Another one was Abhimanyu, who had learned it from his father Arjuna when he was still in his mother's womb.

Abhimanyu had heard his father narrating how to enter the Chakravyuha when he was still an unborn baby. He had listened with curiosity and interest and had memorised everything that his father had said. However, he did not hear how to exit from it because his mother Subhadra had fallen asleep while listening to Arjuna's story and had closed her ears with her hands.

This proved to be fatal for Abhimanyu later on.

The Kaurava army formed the Chakravyuha as a trap for Arjuna, who was away from his main army at that time. They hoped to kill him and end the war in their favour. However, they did not know that Abhimanyu also knew how to enter the formation.

When the Pandava army saw the Chakravyuha, they were worried and confused. They did not know how to break it and reach Arjuna. They asked each other if anyone knew the secret of the formation.

Abhimanyu stepped forward and said that he knew how to enter the Chakravyuha, but not how to exit from it. He said that he was willing to take the risk and lead the attack. He asked his uncles and other warriors to follow him and support him.

The Pandavas were amazed and proud of Abhimanyu's bravery and confidence. They agreed to follow him and help him. They praised him and blessed him.

Abhimanyu then charged towards the Chakravyuha with his chariot, bow, and arrows. He pierced through the first layer of the formation with ease. He then pierced through the second layer, then the third, then the fourth, and so on. He killed many Kaurava soldiers on his way and created havoc in their ranks.

He reached the seventh and final layer of the formation, where he faced the most powerful and experienced warriors of the Kaurava army. They were Dronacharya, Karna, Duryodhana, Dushasana, Ashwatthama, Kripacharya, and Jayadratha. They were all angry and afraid of Abhimanyu's prowess. They decided to gang up on him and kill him by any means possible.

They attacked Abhimanyu from all sides with their weapons and magic. They broke his bow, his arrows, his sword, his shield, his chariot, and his horses. They wounded him with their spears, arrows, maces, and clubs. They surrounded him and prevented him from escaping.

Abhimanyu fought back with all his strength and courage. He used whatever weapons he could find on the battlefield: a wheel, a mace, a sword, a spear. He killed many enemies and wounded many others. He defended himself from their attacks with his skill and agility.

He remembered his father Arjuna, his mother Subhadra, his wife Uttara, his uncle Krishna, and his grandfather Indra. He prayed to them for their help and protection.

He also remembered his duty as a warrior and a prince. He did not give up or surrender. He did not fear death or pain.

He fought till his last breath.

He died a glorious death.

He died a martyr's death.

He died a hero's death.

His death shocked and saddened everyone who heard about it. His father Arjuna was heartbroken and furious. He vowed to avenge his son's death by killing all those who had killed him. His mother Subhadra was devastated and inconsolable. She cursed herself for falling asleep while listening to Arjuna's story. His wife Uttara was grief-stricken and terrified. She feared for her unborn child who was still in her womb.

His uncle Krishna was moved and proud. He praised Abhimanyu for his valour and sacrifice. He assured Uttara that her child would be safe and would become a great king in the future.

His grandfather Indra was pleased and honoured. He welcomed Abhimanyu to his heaven as his son Varchas who had returned to him after sixteen years.

Abhimanyu's story is one of the most inspiring and tragic stories in Hindu mythology and Indian literature. It is a story of bravery, loyalty, honour, duty, love, faith, destiny, and sacrifice.

It is a story that teaches us many lessons about life and death.

It is a story that we should never forget.

Menaka: A Gorgeous Dancer's Temptation and Renunciation

A long time ago, in ancient India, there was a beautiful and talented dancer named Menaka. She was one of the apsaras, the heavenly nymphs who entertained the gods and goddesses in their celestial abode. She was born from the churning of the ocean by the gods and demons, who were looking for the nectar of immortality. She was gifted with incomparable beauty, grace, charm, and skill. She could enchant anyone with her dance and music.

Menaka was also a loyal servant of Indra, the king of the gods. She obeyed his orders without question and did whatever he asked her to do. Sometimes, Indra would send her to earth to seduce and distract some powerful sages or kings who were threatening his authority or supremacy. Menaka would use her charms to lure them away from their penance or duty and make them fall in love with her. Then, she would leave them and return to heaven, leaving them heartbroken and helpless.

Menaka did not mind doing this job for Indra. She did not feel any guilt or remorse for breaking the hearts of her lovers. She did not care about their feelings or fate. She did not have any attachment or emotion for anyone. She only enjoyed her life as an apsara, dancing and singing for the gods and goddesses.

However, everything changed when she met Vishwamitra.

Vishwamitra was one of the most respected and revered sages in ancient India. He was originally a king named Kaushika, who ruled over a vast kingdom with justice and wisdom. He was also a brave warrior who fought many battles and conquered many lands. He had everything that a king could desire: wealth, power, fame, glory, and happiness.

But he was not satisfied with his life as a king. He wanted to become a brahmarishi, the highest rank of sages who had attained supreme knowledge and power. He wanted to surpass even Vashishta, his guru and rival, who was already a brahmarishi. He wanted to challenge Indra himself, who was afraid of his ambition and potential.

So he renounced his kingdom and family and became a hermit. He went to the forest and practised severe penance for many years. He performed many rituals and sacrifices. He meditated on the supreme reality. He gained many divine powers and blessings.

He also faced many obstacles and temptations from Indra, who tried to stop him from achieving his goal. Indra sent many apsaras to seduce him and break his concentration. But Vishwamitra resisted them all with his willpower and determination.

He rejected Rambha, Urvashi, Tilottama, Pramlocha, Ghritachi, Punjikasthala, Swayamprabha, Ruchi, Manorama, Misrakeshi, Sumukhi, Keshini, Madhura, Alambusha, Anjana, Vapu, Vishala, Hemavati, Suvahu, Surasa, Surabhi, Supriya, Suvarna,

and many others.

He also rejected Menaka.

Menaka was sent by Indra to seduce Vishwamitra when he was performing a very difficult penance on the banks of the river Kaushiki. Indra told Menaka that Vishwamitra was the toughest target he had ever given her and that she had to succeed at any cost.

Menaka accepted the challenge and went to earth with confidence and curiosity. She had heard a lot about Vishwamitra's fame and power. She wanted to see him for herself and test his resolve.

She reached the place where Vishwamitra was sitting in meditation under a tree. She saw him as a handsome man with long hair and beard, wearing a deer skin and a rosary around his neck. He had a radiant aura around him that showed his spiritual strength.

Menaka felt a strange attraction towards him that she had never felt before for anyone. She wondered if he would notice her or ignore her like he had done with other apsaras.

She decided to try her best to win his attention and affection.

She transformed herself into a beautiful maiden dressed in fine clothes and jewels. She carried a veena (a musical instrument) in her hands and sang sweetly as she walked towards him.

She reached near him and greeted him respectfully. She said that she was a traveller who had lost her way in the forest and that she needed his help and guidance. She asked him if he could spare some time for her and listen to her music.

Vishwamitra opened his eyes and saw her. He was stunned by her beauty and grace. He felt a surge of desire and passion in his heart. He forgot his penance and his goal. He smiled at her and invited her to sit with him.

Menaka was delighted by his response. She sat next to him and played her veena. She sang songs of love and longing. She looked at him with admiration and affection.

Vishwamitra listened to her music and felt enchanted by her voice. He looked at her with appreciation and attraction.

He asked her who she was and where she came from. He asked her what she wanted from him.

Menaka told him that she was a princess who had left her kingdom in search of true love. She told him that she had wandered all over the world but had not found anyone who could match her heart and soul. She told him that she had fallen in love with him at first sight and that he was the one she had been looking for.

She asked him if he felt the same way for her. She asked him if he would accept her as his wife and companion.

Vishwamitra was moved by her words and touched by her sincerity. He felt a deep connection with her and a genuine love for her. He agreed to marry her and live with her.

He took her hand and kissed it. He put a garland of flowers around her neck. He declared that she was his wife and that he was her husband.

They embraced each other and kissed each other.

They spent many days and nights together in blissful happiness. They forgot everything else in the world. They forgot their duties and responsibilities. They forgot their identities and destinies.

They only remembered their love for each other.

They lived like this for ten years.

However, their happiness was short-lived. Soon after their marriage, Menaka became pregnant with Vishwamitra's child. She was overjoyed by this news and told Vishwamitra about it.

Vishwamitra was also happy at first, but then he realised what he had done. He remembered his penance and his goal. He remembered that he had been tricked by Indra, who had sent Menaka to seduce him. He realised that he had wasted his time and energy on a woman who was not his true partner, but a tool of his enemy.

He became angry and ashamed of himself. He blamed Menaka for his downfall. He accused her of being a liar and a cheat. He said that she did not love him, but only wanted to ruin him.

He then cursed her to be separated from him forever. He said that he did not want her or their child in his life. He said that he would resume his penance and achieve his goal.

He then left her alone in the forest without any care or concern.

Menaka was heartbroken by Vishwamitra's words and actions. She loved him sincerely and deeply. She did not want to harm him or betray him. She wanted to be with him as his wife and mother of his child.

She tried to stop him from leaving her, but he did not listen to her. He pushed her away and walked away from her.

She cried and begged him to come back, but he did not turn back.

She then realised that he was gone forever, and that she had lost him.

She decided to leave the forest and return to heaven. She did not want to stay in a place where she had no love or respect. She also did not want to raise her child in a place where he or she would have no father or family.

She took her unborn child with her and went back to Indra's court. She told Indra what had happened and asked him to forgive her for failing in her mission.

Indra was surprised and sorry for Menaka. He had not expected her to fall in love with Vishwamitra. He had not intended to hurt her or separate her from him. He said that he was proud of her for being brave and honest. He said that he would take care of her and her child.

He then welcomed her back to heaven as one of his apsaras. He gave her a place of honour and respect among the other nymphs. He also gave her many gifts and comforts.

He also promised her that he would find a suitable husband for her, who would love her and cherish her.

Menaka thanked Indra for his kindness and generosity. She accepted his gifts and comforts. She also agreed to marry someone else, if he found someone worthy of her.

She then resumed her life as an apsara, entertaining the gods and goddesses with her dance and music.

However, she was not happy or satisfied. She missed Vishwamitra and their child. She wondered what had happened to them and if they ever thought of her.

She felt lonely and empty inside.

She realised that she had made a mistake by leaving them behind. She realised that she had given up the most precious thing in her life: love.

She decided to renounce her life as an apsara and seek Vishwamitra again. She hoped that he would forgive her and accept her again. She hoped that he would love her and their child again.

She left heaven and came back to earth. She searched for Vishwamitra in the forest, but she could not find him. She learned that he had moved to another place, where he was continuing his penance.

She followed him to his new place, where she saw him sitting under a tree, meditating with his eyes closed. He looked older and thinner than before, but also more radiant and powerful than before.

He had achieved his goal of creating another heaven, which he called Trishanku's heaven, after a king whom he had helped to ascend there alive. He had also become a brahmarshi, the highest rank of sages, after being acknowledged by his teacher Vashishta.

He had also forgotten about Menaka and their child. He had no memories or feelings for them. He had no attachments or distractions. He had only one focus: his penance.

Menaka approached him with love and reverence. She greeted him with respect and admiration. She reminded him of their past relationship and their present situation. She asked him to forgive her and take her back as his wife. She also asked him to accept their child as his son or daughter.

Vishwamitra opened his eyes and saw Menaka standing before him. He did not recognize her or remember anything about her. He felt nothing for her or their child. He was indifferent and detached from them.

He asked her who she was and what she wanted from him. He said that he had no interest in worldly affairs or relationships. He said that he had only one purpose: his penance.

He then asked her to leave him alone and let him continue his meditation.

Menaka was shocked and saddened by Vishwamitra's words and attitude. She realised that he had changed completely, and that there was no hope for them. She realised that he did not love her or their child, and that he never would.

She then decided to leave him alone and let him continue his penance

She then left him alone in the forest without any care or concern.

She cried and wished him well, but she did not turn back.

She then realised that she was alone forever, and that she had lost him.

She decided to leave the earth and return to heaven. She did not want to stay in a place where she had no love or respect. She also did not want to raise their child in a place where he or she would have no father or family.

She took their unborn child with her and went back to Indra's court. She told Indra what had happened and asked him to forgive her for leaving him again.

Indra was surprised and sorry for Menaka again. He had not expected Vishwamitra to reject her again. He had not intended to hurt her or separate them again. He said that he was proud of her for being brave and honest again.

He said that he would take care of her and their child again. He welcomed her back to heaven as one of his apsaras. He gave her a place of honour and respect among the other nymphs. He also gave her many gifts and comforts.

He also promised her that he would find a suitable husband for her, who would love her and cherish her.

Menaka thanked Indra for his kindness and generosity. She accepted his gifts and comforts. She also agreed to marry someone else, if he found someone worthy of her.

She then resumed her life as an apsara, entertaining the gods and goddesses with her dance and music.

However, she was not happy or satisfied. She missed Vishwamitra and their child. She wondered what had happened to them and if they ever thought of her.

She felt lonely and empty inside.

She realised that she had made a mistake by leaving them behind. She realised that she had given up the most precious thing in her life: love.

She decided to renounce her life as an apsara and seek Vishwamitra again. She hoped that he would forgive her and accept her again. She hoped that he would love her and their child again.

She left heaven and came back to earth. She searched for Vishwamitra in the forest, but she could not find him. She learned that he had attained the highest state of enlightenment, which was beyond the reach of any mortal or immortal being. He had become one with the supreme reality, which was beyond any name or form.

He had transcended his penance and his goal. He had transcended his anger and his shame. He had transcended his love and his hate.

He had transcended himself.

Menaka was awed and humbled by Vishwamitra's achievement. She realised that he had reached a level of existence that was beyond her comprehension or imagination. She realised that he had no need for her or their child, or anyone or anything else.

She realised that he was free from all bonds and attachments.

She realised that he was happy and peaceful.

She then decided to leave him alone and let him be in his bliss.

She then left him alone in the forest without any care or concern.

She cried and wished him well, but she did not turn back.

She then realised that she was alone forever, and that she had lost him.

She decided to leave the earth and return to heaven. She did not want to stay in a place where she had no love or respect. She also did not want to raise their child in a place where he or she would have no father or family.

She took their unborn child with her and went back to Indra's court. She told Indra what had happened and asked him to forgive her for leaving him again.

Indra was surprised and sorry for Menaka again. He had not expected Vishwamitra to reach such a high state of enlightenment. He had not intended to hurt her or separate them again. He said that he was proud of her for being brave and honest again. He said that he would take care of her and their child again. He welcomed her back to heaven as one of his apsaras. He gave her a place of honour and respect among the other nymphs. He also gave her many gifts and comforts.

He also told her that he had found a suitable husband for her, who would love her and cherish her. He said that he was a king named Pururava, who was handsome, noble, generous, and wise. He said that he was also a descendant of Ila, the daughter of Manu, the first human being on earth. He said that Pururava was looking for a wife who would share his life and rule with him.

He asked Menaka if she would marry Pururava and become his queen.

Menaka looked at Indra with gratitude and trust. She said that she would marry Pururava and become his queen. She said that she hoped that Pururava would be a good husband for her and a good father for their child.

Indra smiled and nodded. He said that he was sure that Pururava would be a good husband for her and a good father for their child. He said that he would arrange their marriage soon.

He then took Menaka to meet Pururava, who was waiting for them in another hall of heaven.

Pururava saw Menaka and fell in love with her at first sight. He was enchanted by her beauty and grace. He greeted her with respect and admiration. He praised her for her achievements and virtues. He asked her to be his wife and queen.

Menaka saw Pururava and felt a spark of attraction for him. She was impressed by his appearance and personality. She greeted him with warmth and courtesy. She thanked him for his compliments and proposals. She agreed to be his wife and queen.

They exchanged vows of love and loyalty. They blessed each other with happiness and prosperity.

They then had a grand wedding ceremony in heaven, with the gods and goddesses as their guests. They celebrated their union with joy and gratitude.

They then went to Pururavas kingdom on earth, where they lived as king and queen. They were very happy together and looked forward to having children.

They had many children, who inherited their qualities and made them proud.

They ruled their kingdom with justice and generosity. They were loved and respected by their people and allies.

They also remained faithful and devoted to each other. They never forgot their past lovers, but they did not regret their present choices.

They realised that they had found true partners who loved them for who they were, not just for their beauty or skills.

They realised that they had found true happiness and satisfaction.

They realised that they had found true love.

Menaka's story is one of the most romantic and realistic stories in Hindu mythology and Indian literature. It is a story of beauty, talent, temptation, renunciation, love, duty, destiny, and sacrifice.

It is a story that teaches us many lessons about life and love.

It is a story that we should always remember.

Vishwakarma: A Creative Architect's Inventions and Innovations

A long time ago, in ancient India, there was a brilliant and creative architect named Vishwakarma. He was one of the devas, the celestial beings who lived in the heavenly realm of Svarga. He was the son of Prabhasa Vasu, one of the eight Vasus who were the attendants of

Indra, the king of gods. He was also the father of Sanjna, Vishvarupa, Barhismati, Chitrangada, and Nala, who were all famous and influential in their own ways.

Vishwakarma was known as the divine craftsman and engineer of the devas. He designed and built many marvellous things for them, such as their palaces, chariots, weapons, ornaments, and clothes. He also created many wonders for the earth and its inhabitants, such as the mountains, rivers, forests, animals, and plants. He was skilled in all kinds of arts and sciences, such as architecture, sculpture, painting, metallurgy, astronomy, astrology, mathematics, medicine, music, and magic.

He was also curious and adventurous. He always wanted to learn new things and explore new possibilities. He experimented with different materials and methods. He invented new devices and techniques. He improved existing products and processes. He solved problems and challenges. He inspired others with his ideas and innovations.

He was also generous and benevolent. He shared his knowledge and resources with others. He helped those who needed his assistance. He protected those who were in danger. He respected those who deserved his admiration. He loved those who were close to his heart.

He was also humble and devout. He acknowledged his limitations and mistakes. He sought guidance from his elders and teachers. He worshipped his ancestors and gods. He followed his dharma or duty as a deva.

He was also loyal and courageous. He supported his friends and allies. He fought against his enemies and rivals. He defended his rights and interests. He faced his fears and risks.

He was a multifaceted personality who had many achievements and adventures in his life.

Here are some of the stories that illustrate his inventions and innovations:

The Creation of the Universe

According to some versions of Hindu mythology, Vishwakarma was the first being to emerge from the primordial chaos that existed before the creation of the universe. He was endowed with supreme intelligence and power by Brahman, the ultimate reality that pervades everything.

He then used his creative abilities to fashion the universe out of nothingness. He divided it into three realms: heaven (Svarga), earth (Bhumi), and underworld (Patala). He then populated them with various kinds of beings: gods (devas), humans (manavas), demons (asuras), spirits (yakshas), animals (pashus), plants (vanaspati), etc.

He also established the laws of nature that governed the universe: time (kala), space (desha), motion (gati), causation (karma), etc.

He then assigned different roles and functions to different beings according to their qualities (gunas) and actions (karmas). He made Indra the king of gods, Varuna the lord of water, Agni the god of fire, Vayu the god of wind, Surya the sun god, Chandra the moon god, etc.

He also made himself the chief architect and engineer of the universe. He became responsible for maintaining and repairing it whenever it was needed.

He thus became known as Vishwakarma or "the maker of all".

The Creation of Lanka

According to the epic Ramayana , Vishwakarma once created a magnificent city called Lanka for Kubera , the god of wealth and treasure. It was located on an island in the Indian Ocean . It was made of gold , silver , gems , pearls , coral , ivory , wood , metal , stone , etc . It had many palaces , temples , gardens , ponds , bridges , gates , towers , etc . It had many facilities , amenities , luxuries , pleasures , etc . It had many defences , weapons , guards , spies , etc . It was a city that fulfilled all desires .

However , Kubera's half-brother Ravana , who was a powerful demon king , coveted Lanka for himself . He attacked Kubera with his army of demons . Kubera fled to Mount Kailash , where he sought refuge with Lord Shiva . Ravana then occupied Lanka as his capital . He ruled over it with tyranny and arrogance . He also abducted Sita , the wife of Lord Rama , who was an avatar of Lord Vishnu . This led to the war between Rama and Ravana , in which Rama was assisted by Hanuman , the monkey god , and his army of monkeys and bears .

During the war , Rama's army tried to cross the ocean to reach Lanka . However , they faced many obstacles and dangers . They then prayed to Lord Shiva for help . Shiva then instructed Vishwakarma to build a bridge across the ocean . Vishwakarma agreed and used his skills and tools to construct a bridge made of rocks , trees , and vines . He also used his magic to make it strong and stable . He then named it Rama Setu or "Rama's Bridge" .

Rama's army then crossed the bridge and reached Lanka . They fought against Ravana's army and defeated them . Rama then killed Ravana and rescued Sita . He then returned to his kingdom of Ayodhya with Sita and his allies . He then thanked Vishwakarma for his help and praised him for his work .

Vishwakarma then returned to heaven with his tools and magic . He then became known as Setubandha or "the builder of bridges" .

The Creation of Dwaraka

According to the epic Mahabharata , Vishwakarma once created a splendid city called Dwaraka for Lord Krishna , who was an avatar of Lord Vishnu . It was located on the western coast of India . It was made of crystal , marble , gold , silver , gems , pearls , coral , ivory , wood , metal , stone , etc . It had many palaces , temples , gardens , ponds , bridges , gates , towers , etc . It had many facilities , amenities , luxuries , pleasures , etc . It had many defences , weapons , guards , spies , etc . It was a city that protected all virtues .

Krishna lived in Dwaraka with his wives, children, friends, relatives, and followers. He ruled over it with justice and compassion. He also helped the Pandavas, who were his cousins, in their righteous war against the Kauravas, who were their evil cousins. He also performed many miracles and taught many lessons to his devotees.

Okay, I will generate a story based on Hindu mythology and Indian literature, which is elaborate and extensive for a 25-30 minutes reading. The title of the story is "Vishwakarma: A Creative Architect's Inventions and Innovations". I will also include a lot of factual information, all the necessary details, and tailor the story for readers of the age 8-15. Here is the story:

A long time ago, in ancient India, there was a brilliant and creative architect named Vishwakarma. He was one of the devas, the celestial beings who lived in the heavenly realm of Svarga. He was the son of

Prabhasa Vasu, one of the eight Vasus who were the attendants of Indra, the king of gods. He was also the father of Sanjna, Vishvarupa, Barhismati, Chitrangada, and Nala, who were all famous and influential figures in Hindu mythology

Vishwakarma was the divine craftsman and engineer of the devas. He designed and built their palaces, chariots, weapons, and ornaments. He also created many wonders and marvels in the universe, such as the earth, the sky, the sun, the moon, and the stars. He was skilled in all kinds of arts and sciences, such as architecture, sculpture, metallurgy, astronomy, astrology, and magic. He was also a master of Vedas, the ancient sacred texts of Hinduism. He was revered and respected by all for his wisdom and talent

Vishwakarma had many amazing inventions and innovations that changed the course of history and mythology. Some of them are:

- The Vajra: The Vajra was a thunderbolt-like weapon that was wielded by Indra. It was made from the bones of Dadhichi, a sage who sacrificed his life for the cause of the devas. Vishwakarma shaped and sharpened the bones into a powerful weapon that could destroy any enemy or obstacle. The Vajra was used by Indra to defeat many demons and enemies, such as Vritra, Bali, Shushna, Namuchi, and others. It was also used by Indra to split open mountains and release rivers. The Vajra was one of the most feared and revered weapons in Hindu mythology

- The Pushpaka Vimana: The Pushpaka Vimana was a flying chariot that could travel anywhere in the world. It was made from gold and jewels and had many rooms and facilities. It could accommodate hundreds of people and could change its shape and size according to the wish of its owner. Vishwakarma built it for Kubera, the god of wealth and treasure. However, it was later stolen by Ravana, the king of Lanka and the main antagonist of Ramayana. Ravana used it to abduct Sita, the wife of Rama, an avatar of Vishnu. Rama later defeated Ravana in a war and recovered Sita and the Pushpaka Vimana. He then returned it to Kubera as a gesture of gratitude and friendship. The Pushpaka Vimana was one of the most advanced and luxurious vehicles in Hindu mythology.

- The Shiva Lingam: The Shiva Lingam was a symbol of Shiva, one of the three supreme gods in Hinduism. It represented his cosmic energy and creative power. It was shaped like an oval stone with a cylindrical base. Vishwakarma created it from fire during a contest between Brahma, Vishnu, and Shiva to prove their supremacy. Vishwakarma made a pillar of fire that reached from heaven to earth and challenged Brahma and Vishnu to find its ends. Brahma took the form of a swan and flew upwards to find the top end while Vishnu took the form of a boar and dug downwards to find the bottom end. However, neither could find any end as the pillar kept extending infinitely in both directions. They realised that it was an illusion created by Shiva to test them. They then praised Shiva as the greatest among them and worshipped him as a lingam made from fire. Vishwakarma then cooled down the fire lingam into a stone lingam that became an icon of Shiva worship in Hinduism. The Shiva Lingam was one of the most sacred and mysterious objects in Hindu mythology.

- The Cities of Lanka, Dwaraka, and Indraprastha: Vishwakarma also built many magnificent cities for various kings and gods in Hindu mythology. Some of them are:
  - Lanka: Lanka was an island city that was ruled by Ravana, who had obtained it from Kubera by force. It was made from gold and silver and had many palaces, gardens, temples, and fortifications. It was surrounded by the ocean and protected by many magical and natural barriers. It was considered to be one of the most beautiful and prosperous cities in the world. However, it was also the scene of many evil deeds and crimes committed by Ravana and his allies. It was eventually destroyed by Rama and his army of monkeys and bears in the war against Ravana.

  - Dwaraka: Dwaraka was a coastal city that was ruled by Krishna, an avatar of Vishnu and the main protagonist of Mahabharata. It was made from crystal and coral and had many palaces, gardens, temples, and harbours. It was surrounded by the sea and protected by many divine and natural barriers. It was considered to be one of the most holy and peaceful cities in the world. It was also the home of many heroes and sages who participated in the Kurukshetra War, such as Arjuna, Bhima, Draupadi, Yudhishthira, Balarama, Satyaki, Kunti, Subhadra, Abhimanyu, and others. It was eventually submerged by the sea after Krishna's departure from the world.

- ○ Indraprastha: Indraprastha was a capital city that was ruled by Yudhishthira, the eldest of the Pandava brothers and the main protagonist of Mahabharata. It was made from wood and stone and had many palaces, gardens, temples, and courts. It was located on the banks of the Yamuna river and protected by many natural and human barriers. It was considered to be one of the most righteous and prosperous cities in the world. It was also the site of many events and episodes in Mahabharata, such as the Rajasuya Yajna, the game of dice, the exile of the Pandavas, the return of the Pandavas, the Kurukshetra War, and others. It was eventually abandoned by Yudhishthira after his coronation as the emperor of Bharata.

These cities were some of the most remarkable and legendary creations of Vishwakarma in Hindu mythology.

Vishwakarma's story is one of the most fascinating and inspiring stories in Hindu mythology and Indian literature. It is a story of creativity, innovation, invention, artistry, engineering, architecture, science, magic, wisdom, and talent.

It is a story that teaches us many lessons about life and work.

It is a story that we should always admire.

Tenali Raman: A Witty Jester's Humor and Intelligence

A long time ago, in ancient India, there was a witty and intelligent jester named Tenali Raman. He was one of the eight poets or Ashtadiggajas in the court of King Krishnadevaraya, who ruled the Vijayanagara Empire from 1509 to 1529 CE. He wrote poems in Telugu and was famous for his humour and sharpness. He was also known as Tenali Ramakrishna or Tenali Ramalinga. He was born in a village called Tenali in Andhra Pradesh and belonged to a Niyogi Brahmin family.

Tenali Raman had many amusing and interesting stories that showed his wit and wisdom. Some of them are:

- How Tenali Raman Became a Court Poet: Tenali Raman was not always a court poet. He was once a poor and ordinary man who had a great desire to learn and become famous. He heard that King Krishnadevaraya was looking for talented poets to join his court. He decided to go to Vijayanagara and try his luck.

He reached Vijayanagara and saw that it was a magnificent city with many palaces, temples, gardens, and markets. He also saw that it was crowded with many people from different regions, religions, and professions. He felt excited and curious about the city.

He then went to the royal palace and asked for an audience with the king. He said that he was a poet who wanted to serve the king. The guards laughed at him and said that he did not look like a poet. They said that he looked like a beggar. They mocked him and drove him away.

Tenali Raman felt insulted and angry. He decided to teach them a lesson. He went to a nearby temple and prayed to Goddess Kali for her help. He then saw a priest coming out of the temple with a plate of offerings. He quickly snatched the plate from the priest and ran away.

The priest shouted and chased him. The guards heard the commotion and joined the chase. They caught Tenali Raman and brought him to the king.

The king asked him why he had stolen the offerings from the temple. Tenali Raman said that he had not stolen anything, but had only taken what was his right. He said that he was a poet who had composed a poem in praise of Goddess Kali, and that she had rewarded him with the offerings.

The king asked him to recite his poem. Tenali Raman recited his poem, which was clever and humorous. It went like this:

O Kali, you are the mother of all, You are the giver of boons small and tall. You are the destroyer of evil and sin, You are the protector of virtue and kin. You are the source of power and grace, You are the ruler of time and space. You are the lover of Shiva, your consort, You are the master of life, death, and sport. You are the one who fulfils every wish, You are the one who grants every dish. You are the one who knows every art, You are the one who owns every heart. You are the one who likes every rhyme, You are the one who rewards every time.

The king and everyone else in the court were impressed by Tenali Raman's poem. They praised him for his talent and creativity. The king asked him how he had learned to compose such poems.

Tenali Raman said that he had learned from his teacher, who was none other than Goddess Kali herself. He said that she had appeared in his dream one night and had taught him everything about poetry.

The king was amazed by Tenali Raman's story. He thought that he was indeed blessed by Goddess Kali. He decided to appoint him as one of his court poets.

He gave him a gold chain as a token of his appreciation. He also gave him a house near the palace where he could live comfortably.

Tenali Raman thanked the king for his generosity and kindness. He also thanked Goddess Kali for her help and guidance.

He then became one of the most famous and respected poets in King Krishnadevaraya's court.

The moral of this story is: If you have talent and faith, you can achieve anything in life.

- How Tenali Raman Saved His Son from Death: Tenali Raman had a son named Bhaskara, who was very dear to him. He loved him more than anything else in the world. He taught him many things and took care of him.

One day, Bhaskara fell ill with a fever. He became very weak and pale. Tenali Raman was worried and took him to a doctor. The doctor examined him and said that he had a serious infection in his blood. He said that he needed a rare herb called Sanjeevani, which could cure any disease. He said that the herb grew only on a mountain called Meru, which was far away from Vijayanagara.

He said that it was very difficult to get the herb, as the mountain was guarded by many dangers and obstacles. He said that only a brave and clever person could get the herb.

Tenali Raman was determined to save his son's life. He decided to go to the mountain and get the herb. He packed some food and clothes and set off on his journey.

He reached the foot of the mountain after many days of travel. He saw that it was very high and steep. He also saw that it was surrounded by many wild animals, such as lions, tigers, bears, snakes, and scorpions.

He did not lose hope or courage. He used his wit and intelligence to avoid or overcome the animals. He threw stones at them, made noises to scare them, or hid behind rocks or trees.

He climbed the mountain with great difficulty and reached the top. He saw that there was a beautiful garden with many flowers and fruits. He also saw that there was a small hut where a sage lived.

He went to the hut and greeted the sage with respect and humility. He said that he had come to get the Sanjeevani herb for his son, who was dying of a fever.

The sage looked at him with compassion and kindness. He said that he had the Sanjeevani herb in his garden, but he could not give it to him easily. He said that he had to test him first.

He said that he would ask him three questions, and if he answered them correctly, he would give him the herb. But if he answered them wrongly, he would have to leave without the herb.

Tenali Raman agreed to take the test. He said that he was ready for the questions.

The sage asked him the first question:

What is more precious than gold?

Tenali Raman thought for a while and answered:

Knowledge is more precious than gold.

The sage nodded and asked him the second question:

What is more powerful than fire?

Tenali Raman thought for a while and answered:

Love is more powerful than fire.

The sage nodded again and asked him the third question:

What is more beautiful than flowers?

Tenali Raman thought for a while and answered:

Life is more beautiful than flowers.

The sage smiled and clapped his hands. He said that he had answered all the questions correctly. He praised him for his wisdom and understanding.

He then gave him the Sanjeevani herb and wished him well.

Tenali Raman thanked him for his generosity and blessing. He then took the herb and ran down the mountain.

He reached Vijayanagar after many days of travel. He gave the herb to his son and cured him of his fever.

He hugged his son and kissed him. He thanked Goddess Kali for her help and protection.

He then lived happily with his son and wife.

The moral of this story is: If you have love and knowledge, you can overcome any difficulty in life.

- How Tenali Raman Outwitted a Thief: Tenali Raman had a lot of money and jewels, which he had earned from his poetry and service to the king. He kept them in a chest in his house, which he locked with a strong key.

One night, a thief came to his house and tried to break into his chest. He used a crowbar, a hammer, a chisel, and a saw to open the lock. But he could not succeed, as the lock was too strong.

He then decided to take away the whole chest with him. He lifted it on his shoulders and walked out of the house.

But as soon as he stepped out of the house, he heard a voice behind him saying:

"Hey, thief! Where are you going with my chest?"

He turned around and saw Tenali Raman standing at the door with a lamp in his hand.

He was shocked and scared. He dropped the chest and ran away as fast as he could.

Tenali Raman laughed loudly and picked up his chest. He then went back inside his house and locked his door.

He then slept peacefully with his money and jewels safe in his chest.

The next day, he told everyone about how he had outwitted a thief who had tried to rob him.

Everyone was amazed and curious about how he had done it.

They asked him how he had known that there was a thief in his house.

Tenali Raman said that he had not known it at first. He said that he had been sleeping soundly when he heard a loud noise coming from his chest. He said that he had woken up and seen the thief trying to break into his chest. He said that he had pretended to be asleep and waited for the right moment to catch him.

They asked him how he had caught him.

Tenali Raman said that he had used his wit and intelligence to catch him. He said that he had known that the thief would not be able to open the lock, as it was too strong. He said that he had also known that the thief would try to take away the whole chest with him, as it was too heavy to carry. He said that he had then thought of a clever plan to stop him.

He said that he had tied a long rope to his chest and hidden it under his bed. He said that he had also tied a bell to the other end of the rope and hung it near his door. He said that he had then waited for the thief to lift the chest and walk out of the house.

He said that as soon as the thief had lifted the chest, the rope had pulled the bell and made a ringing sound. He said that he had then woken up and acted as if he had seen the thief for the first time. He said that he had then shouted at him and scared him away.

He said that this way, he had saved his chest and his money.

They asked him how he had thought of such a clever plan.

Tenali Raman said that he had learned from his teacher, who was none other than Goddess Kali herself. He said that she had appeared in his dream one night and had taught him everything about wit and intelligence.

He then recited a poem in praise of Goddess Kali, which went like this:

O Kali, you are the mother of all, You are the giver of boons small and tall. You are the destroyer of evil and sin, You are the protector of virtue and kin. You are the source of power and grace, You are the ruler of time and space. You are the lover of Shiva, your consort, You are the master of life, death, and sport. You are the one who fulfils every wish, You are the one who grants every dish. You are the one who knows every art, You are the one who owns every heart. You are the one who likes every rhyme, You are the one who rewards every time.

Everyone was impressed by Tenali Raman's poem. They praised him for his talent and creativity. They also praised Goddess Kali for her help and guidance.

They then laughed at Tenali Raman's story and enjoyed his humour and intelligence.

The moral of this story is: If you have wit and intelligence, you can outsmart any enemy in life.

Ekalavya: A Loyal Disciple's Dedication and Loss

A long time ago, in ancient India, there was a loyal and dedicated disciple named Ekalavya. He was the son of Prince Devashrava, the brother of Kunti and Vasudeva, who were the parents of the Pandavas and Lord Krishna respectively. This made Ekalavya a cousin of the Pandavas and Krishna. However, he did not know his true identity, as he was abandoned by his father when he was just a baby. He was found and adopted by Hiranyadhanu, the chief of the Nishadas, a tribe of hunters and forest dwellers.

Ekalavya grew up to be a handsome and brave young man. He learned hunting, fishing, tracking, and fighting from his adoptive father and his tribe. He also had a natural talent for archery, which he practised with great passion and devotion. He dreamed of becoming a great archer like Arjuna, the third of the Pandava brothers, who was famous for his skill and prowess with the bow and arrow.

One day, he heard that Dronacharya, the royal guru of Hastinapura, was teaching archery to the Kauravas and the Pandavas in a nearby forest. He was curious and eager to learn from him. He decided to go to the forest and request Dronacharya to accept him as his student.

He reached the forest and saw Dronacharya teaching archery to his students. He was amazed by his knowledge and expertise. He also saw Arjuna and his brothers practising with their bows and arrows. He was impressed by their skill and grace.

He approached Dronacharya and bowed to him with respect. He introduced himself as Ekalavya, the son of Hiranya Dhanu, the chief of the Nishadas. He expressed his desire to learn archery from him.

Dronacharya looked at him with surprise and suspicion. He asked him why he wanted to learn archery. Ekalavya said that he wanted to become a great archer like Arjuna. He said that he admired Arjuna and considered him as his role model.

Dronacharya smiled and said that Arjuna was indeed a great archer, but he was also a Kshatriya, a member of the warrior caste. He said that Ekalavya was not a Kshatriya, but a Shudra, a member of the lowest caste. He said that Shudras were not allowed to learn archery or any other martial art. He said that it was against the rules of society and religion.

He then refused to accept Ekalavya as his student. He told him to go back to his tribe and live according to his caste duties.

Ekalavya felt hurt and disappointed by Dronacharya's words. He felt that it was unfair and unjust to deny him education based on his birth. He felt that he had the right to learn archery as much as anyone else.

He did not argue or protest with Dronacharya. He respected him as a guru and accepted his decision.

He then left the forest with a heavy heart.

However, he did not give up on his dream of becoming an archer. He decided to learn archery by himself.

He went back to his tribe and made a clay statue of Dronacharya under a large banyan tree near his hut. He considered it as his guru and worshipped it every day.

He then practised archery before the statue every day with dedication and determination. He used wooden sticks as arrows and animal skins as targets. He followed every instruction that he had heard from Dronacharya in the forest.

He believed that if he practised before his guru, he would become an expert archer one day.

He did this for many years without anyone's knowledge or help.

One day, Dronacharya and his students went to the same forest for hunting. They were accompanied by their dog, who ran ahead of them.

The dog reached Ekalavya's hut and saw him practising archery before his statue. The dog started barking loudly at him.

Ekalavya was annoyed by the dog's noise. He shot seven arrows in quick succession at the dog's mouth without hurting it. The arrows filled the dog's mouth and stopped its barking.

The dog ran back to its owners with arrows in its mouth.

Dronacharya and his students saw the dog and were astonished. They wondered who had shot the arrows and how.

They followed the dog's trail and reached Ekalavya's hut.

They saw Ekalavya standing before his statue with his bow and arrows.

Ekalavya saw them and recognized them. He was overjoyed to see his guru and his role model. He bowed to them with respect and reverence.

He greeted Dronacharya as his guru and Arjuna as his brother. He told them that he had learned archery from them by making a statue of Dronacharya and practising before it.

He also apologised for shooting at their dog. He said that he had done it to stop its barking, which was disturbing his practice.

Dronacharya and his students were amazed and impressed by Ekalavyas story. They praised him for his devotion and skill.

Dronacharya asked him to show his archery skills. Ekalavya agreed and demonstrated his skills. He shot arrows at various targets with speed and accuracy. He hit every target with ease and precision.

Dronacharya and his students were stunned by Ekalavya's performance. They realised that he had surpassed Arjuna in archery.

Arjuna was shocked and jealous. He remembered Dronacharya's promise to make him the greatest archer in the world. He felt that Ekalavya had broken his promise and betrayed him.

He complained to Dronacharya about Ekalavya. He asked him how he could allow a Shudra to learn archery and become better than him.

Dronacharya felt guilty and ashamed. He realised that he had made a mistake by rejecting Ekalavya as his student. He realised that he had been unfair and biassed to him.

He also realised that he had to keep his promise to Arjuna. He decided to do something to make Arjuna the best archer again.

He thought of a way to do it. He asked Ekalavya for his guru dakshina, the fee that a student pays to his teacher after completing his education.

Ekalavya was delighted and honoured by Dronacharya's request. He said that he would give anything that his guru wanted.

Dronacharya asked him to cut off his right thumb and give it to him as guru dakshina.

Ekalavya was shocked and saddened by Dronacharya's demand. He knew that without his right thumb, he would not be able to shoot arrows properly. He knew that he would lose his skill and fame as an archer.

He also knew that it was a cruel and unjust demand from his guru, who had never taught him anything or cared for him.

However, he did not question or refuse Dronacharya's demand. He respected him as a guru and obeyed him as a student.

He took out a knife and cut off his right thumb without any hesitation or complaint. He then gave it to Dronacharya as guru dakshina with a smile on his face.

Dronacharya took the thumb and felt sorry for Ekalavya. He blessed him for his loyalty and courage.

He then left the hut with his students, leaving Ekalavya alone with his statue.

Ekalavya felt pain and loss in his hand and heart. He realised that he had lost his thumb and skill as an archer.

He also realised that he had lost his guru and brother as well.

He cried silently before his statue, which was now stained with his blood.

He then lived in the forest with his tribe, without any fame or glory as an archer.

However, he did not lose hope or faith in himself. He continued to practise archery with his remaining fingers, with dedication and determination.

He believed that if he practised hard enough, he would become an expert archer again one day.

He did this for many years without anyone's knowledge or help.

One day, he heard that there was a great war going on between the Pandavas and the Kauravas in Kurukshetra. He heard that Arjuna was fighting on the side of the Pandavas, while Karna, another great archer, was fighting on the side of the Kauravas.

He decided to go to Kurukshetra and watch the war. He wanted to see Arjuna and Karna in action. He also wanted to see if he could still match them in archery.

He reached Kurukshetra and saw the war going on. He saw thousands of warriors fighting each other with various weapons. He saw bloodshed and death everywhere.

He also saw Arjuna and Karna fighting each other with their bows and arrows. They were both skilled and powerful archers, who matched each other in every aspect.

They shot arrows at each other with speed and accuracy. They hit each other's shields, helmets, armors, and chariots. They also dodged, blocked, or deflected each other's arrows with their skill and agility.

They fought for a long time, without any sign of victory or defeat.

Ekalavya watched them with awe and admiration. He also watched them with curiosity and challenge. He wondered if he could still shoot arrows as well as them. He wondered if he could still hit their targets or avoid their attacks.

He decided to test his skills and join the war. He took out his bow and arrows and aimed at Arjuna and Karna. He did not want to harm them or interfere with their duel. He only wanted to see if he could match them in archery.

He shot arrows at them with his remaining fingers, with dedication and determination. He used his wit and intelligence to calculate the distance, speed, angle, and direction of his shots.

He shot arrows at Arjuna's shield, helmet, armour, and chariot. He also shot arrows at Karna's shield, helmet, armour, and chariot.

He hit every target with ease and precision.

Arjuna and Karna were surprised and annoyed by Ekalavya's arrows. They did not know who was shooting at them or why. They thought that it was an enemy or a traitor who wanted to kill them or distract them.

They looked around and saw Ekalavya standing on a hill with his bow and arrows. They recognized him as the Nishada prince who had learned archery from Dronacharya's statue.

They were amazed and impressed by his skills. They realised that he had surpassed them in archery.

They also felt guilty and ashamed of themselves. They remembered how they had treated him in the past. They remembered how Dronacharya had asked for his thumb as guru dakshina and how they had agreed to it. They remembered how they had deprived him of his thumb and skill as an archer.

They realised that they had been unfair and cruel to him.

They decided to apologise to him and make amends with him.

They stopped fighting each other and turned towards Ekalavya. They greeted him with respect and admiration. They praised him for his devotion and skill.

They also apologised to him for their past actions. They said that they were sorry for hurting him and betraying him. They said that they were wrong to judge him by his birth or caste. They said that they were wrong to take away his thumb or skill.

They then asked him to forgive them and accept them as his friends.

Ekalavya was touched and moved by their words. He said that he forgave them and accepted them as his friends. He said that he did not hold any grudge or resentment against them.

He also thanked them for their compliments and apologies.

He then joined them in the war as their ally. He fought on the side of the Pandavas against the Kauravas.

He used his skills and courage to help them win the war.

He also used his skills and grace to save their lives.

He saved Arjuna from Karna's fatal arrow by shooting it down with his own arrow.

He saved Karna from Arjuna's fatal arrow by shooting it down with his own arrow.

He saved both of them from death by sacrificing his own life.

He died a noble death.

He died a hero's death.

His death shocked and saddened everyone who heard about it. His friends Arjuna and Karna were heartbroken and grateful. They vowed to honour his memory and legacy by being good friends and brothers.

His guru Dronacharya was proud and remorseful. He blessed him for his loyalty and courage. He also cursed himself for his mistake and injustice.

His father Hiranyadhanu was proud and sorrowful. He praised him for his devotion and skill. He also mourned him for his loss and sacrifice.

His mother Kunti was proud and joyful. She revealed him as her nephew, the son of her brother Devashrava. She welcomed him as her son, who had returned to her after many years.

She then took him to heaven as one of her sons who had died in the war.

Ekalavyas story is one of the most tragic and inspiring stories in Hindu mythology and Indian literature. It is a story of loyalty, dedication, skill, sacrifice, friendship, forgiveness, justice, injustice, birth, death, caste, class, guru, disciple, thumb, arrow, war, peace, love, hate, life.

It is a story that teaches us many lessons about life and values.

It is a story that we should always remember.

Ghatotkacha: The Unspoken Son of Bhima

A long time ago, in ancient India, there was a brave and powerful warrior named Ghatotkacha. He was the son of Bhima, one of the five Pandava brothers, and Hidimbi, a demoness who lived in the forest. He was half-human and half-demon, which gave him many extraordinary abilities. He could fly in the air, change his size and shape, and perform magic and illusions. He was also very loyal and devoted to his father and his uncles, who were fighting against their cousins, the Kauravas, in the great war of Kurukshetra.

Ghatotkacha's story began when the Pandavas were living in exile in the forest after escaping from a fire trap set by their enemies. One night, they came across a cave where a demon named Hidimba lived with his sister Hidimbi. Hidimba smelled the Pandavas and wanted to eat them. He sent his sister to lure them out of the cave. Hidimbi went to the cave and saw Bhima, who was guarding his brothers while they slept. She was instantly attracted to him and fell in love with him. She told him about her brother's plan and asked him to escape with her. Bhima refused to leave his brothers and decided to fight Hidimba instead. He killed Hidimba in a fierce battle and then agreed to marry Hidimbi at the request of his mother Kunti. He also promised to stay with her until she gave birth to a son.

Soon, Hidimbi gave birth to a son who had a bald head shaped like a pot. They named him Ghatotkacha, which means "pot-headed". Ghatotkacha grew up very fast and became a strong and handsome young man. He learned hunting, fighting, and magic from his mother and her tribe. He also inherited his father's weapon of choice, the mace. He loved his parents very much and respected them as his teachers.

When Ghatotkacha was still a child, Bhima had to leave him and his mother to join his brothers in their quest for justice. He told Ghatotkacha to always obey his mother and help his uncles whenever they needed him. He also told him to be proud of his heritage and use his powers for good. Ghatotkacha promised to follow his father's words and bid him farewell.

Ghatotkacha lived with his mother in the forest until he heard about the war between the Pandavas and the Kauravas. He decided to join the war on the side of the Pandavas and support his father and uncles. He took his mace and flew to Kurukshetra, where the war was taking place.

He reached Kurukshetra and saw that it was a huge battlefield with thousands of warriors fighting each other with various weapons. He also saw that it was divided into two sides: one side was led by

Yudhishthira, the eldest of the Pandavas, who had a white flag with a golden lotus; the other side was led by Duryodhana, the eldest of the Kauravas, who had a red flag with a silver snake.

He joined the Pandava side and met his father Bhima, who was overjoyed to see him. He introduced him to his uncle's Yudhishthira, Arjuna, Nakula, and Sahadeva, who welcomed him warmly. He also met Krishna, who was Arjuna's charioteer and guide, who blessed him with a smile.

He then fought in the war with great courage and skill. He used his mace to smash his enemies' heads and bodies. He used his magic to create illusions and confusion among his foes. He used his flight to attack from above and escape from danger.

He killed many warriors from the Kaurava side, such as Alambusha, Alayudha, Jalasandha, Durmukha, Dushkarna, Vrishasena, Shalya's song Rukmarata, and many others.

He also saved many warriors from the Pandava side, such as Bhima, Arjuna, Satyaki, Drupada, Virata, and many others.

He was especially close to his cousin Abhimanyu, the son of Arjuna and Subhadra, who was also a great warrior. They fought together and protected each other. They also shared their stories and secrets. They were like brothers.

Ghatotkacha was one of the most feared and respected warriors in the war. He caused a lot of damage and destruction to the Kaurava army. He was also one of the most loyal and devoted warriors to the Pandava cause. He followed his father's orders and his uncles' commands. He fought for justice and righteousness.

However, he also faced many challenges and dangers in the war. He had to face many powerful and cunning enemies, such as Karna, Drona, Ashwatthama, Duryodhana, Shakuni, and many others. He had to face many weapons and tricks, such as arrows, spears, swords, axes, clubs, nets, fire, poison, and many others. He had to face many injuries and pains, such as wounds, cuts, bruises, burns, and many others.

He also had to face his own death.

His death came on the fourteenth day of the war, when he faced Karna in a final duel. Karna was one of the greatest archers in the world, who had a divine weapon called the Vasavi Shakti, which could kill any enemy in one shot. He had received this weapon from Indra, the king of gods, who had asked him to use it only against Arjuna.

However, Karna decided to use it against Ghatotkacha instead. He saw that Ghatotkacha was causing a lot of trouble to the Kaurava army with his magic and might. He saw that Ghatotkacha had grown to a gigantic size and was crushing soldiers and chariots under his feet. He saw that Ghatotkacha had created a huge cloud of darkness that covered the sky and made it impossible for anyone to see anything.

He decided that he had to stop Ghatotkacha at any cost. He took out his Vasavi Shakti and aimed it at Ghatotkacha's chest. He invoked its power and released it with a loud shout.

The Vasavi Shakti flew like a lightning bolt towards Ghatotkacha. It pierced through his chest and exploded with a thunderous sound.

Ghatotkacha felt a sharp pain in his chest and a burning sensation in his body. He knew that he had been hit by a fatal weapon. He knew that he was going to die.

He did not cry or scream. He did not curse or regret. He did not fear or despair.

He smiled and thanked Krishna for his life and death. He said that he was happy to die for his father and uncles. He said that he was happy to die by Karna's hand.

He then used his last breath and his last magic to do one final act of service to the Pandavas.

He reduced his size to that of a normal human and fell on Karna's chariot with his full weight.

He crushed Karna's chariot into pieces and killed Karna's charioteer Adhiratha.

He also broke Karna's bow Gandiva and destroyed many of his arrows.

He then died with a smile on his face.

His death shocked and saddened everyone who saw it or heard about it. His father Bhima was heartbroken and furious. He vowed to kill Karna for killing his son. His uncles Yudhishthira, Arjuna, Nakula, and Sahadeva were grief-stricken and grateful. They praised him for his loyalty and courage. His cousin Abhimanyu was devastated and inspired. He decided to follow his example and fight till the end.

His enemy Karna was surprised and remorseful. He realised that he had killed a noble warrior who had sacrificed himself for his family. He also realised that he had wasted his divine weapon on him instead of Arjuna.

His guru Dronacharya was proud and regretful. He blessed him for his devotion and skill. He also cursed himself for his mistake and injustice.

His mother Hidimbi was proud and sorrowful. She praised him for his devotion and skill. She also mourned him for his loss and sacrifice.

His aunt Kunti was proud and joyful. She revealed him as her nephew, the son of her brother Devashrava. She welcomed him as her son, who had returned to her after many years.

She then took him to heaven as one of her sons who had died in the war.

Ghatotkacha's story is one of the most heroic and tragic stories in Hindu mythology and Indian literature. It is a story of loyalty, dedication, skill, sacrifice, friendship, forgiveness, justice, injustice, birth, death, caste, class, guru, disciple, thumb, arrow, war, peace, love, hate, life.

Valmiki: A Transformed Poet's Inspiration and Legacy

A long time ago, in ancient India, there was a transformed poet named Valmiki. He was the author of the Ramayana, one of the most famous and influential epics in Hinduism and world literature. He was also revered as Adi Kavi, the first poet, who invented the Sanskrit verse form called shloka, which was used to compose many other epics and texts. He was also a sage and a teacher, who taught and guided many disciples, including Lava and Kusha, the twin sons of Rama and Sita.

Valmiki's story began when he was not a poet or a sage, but a robber and a murderer. He was born as Ratnakara, the son of a sage named Prachetasa. However, he was separated from his parents when he was young and grew up in the forest with a group of bandits. He became their leader and terrorised the travellers who passed through the forest. He robbed them of their wealth and killed them mercilessly. He did not care about morality or religion. He did not know his true identity or purpose.

One day, he met a sage named Narada, who was travelling through the forest with his musical instrument called veena. Ratnakara saw him and decided to rob him. He stopped him and demanded his valuables. Narada said that he had nothing but his veena and his name. Ratnakara said that he would take his veena and kill him.

Narada asked him why he was doing such evil deeds. Ratnakara said that he was doing it for his family, who depended on him for their survival. Narada asked him if his family would share his sins as well as his wealth. Ratnakara said that they would, as they loved him and supported him.

Narada challenged him to go and ask his family if they would share his sins. Ratnakara agreed to do so, but asked Narada to stay there until he returned. He tied Narada to a tree and went to his home.

He asked his wife and children if they would share his sins. They were shocked and horrified by his question. They said that they would not share his sins, as they were his own responsibility. They said that they only expected him to provide them with food and shelter, not blood and crime.

Ratnakara was stunned and ashamed by their answers. He realised that he had been living a life of ignorance and wickedness. He realised that he had wasted his life in violence and greed.

He returned to Narada with a repentant heart. He untied him and begged for his forgiveness. He asked him how he could redeem himself from his sins.

Narada forgave him and told him that there was still hope for him. He told him that he could attain salvation by meditating on the name of Rama, an avatar of Vishnu, the supreme god of Hinduism.

He taught him how to chant the name of Rama by saying "Mara", which means "die". He told him to repeat it continuously until it became "Rama".

He then left him to meditate under a tree.

Ratnakara followed Narada's instructions and meditated on the name of Rama. He chanted "Mara" over and over again until it became "Rama". He forgot everything else and focused only on Rama.

He meditated for many years without any interruption or distraction.

As he meditated, ants build anthills around him and covered his body completely. Only his eyes were visible from the anthills.

He became known as Valmiki, which means "one born from an anthill".

One day, Narada came back to see him. He saw that he had become a transformed person. He saw that he had attained enlightenment and peace.

He called out to him and asked him to come out of the anthills.

Valmiki came out of the anthills with Narada's help. He greeted Narada with respect and gratitude.

Narada congratulated him for his achievement and blessed him with divine knowledge.

He then told him about Rama's life story, which was full of adventure, romance, tragedy, heroism, morality, spirituality, and divinity.

He told him how Rama was born as the prince of Ayodhya in the kingdom of Kosala; how he married Sita, the princess of Mithila, after breaking the bow of Shiva; how he was exiled to the forest for fourteen years by his father Dasharatha, on the request of his stepmother Kaikeyi; how he travelled across forests and mountains with Sita and his brother Lakshmana; how he befriended many animals and sages, such as Hanuman, Sugriva, Jatayu, Agastya, and others; how he fought many demons and enemies, such as Ravana, Kumbhakarna, Indrajit, Maricha, and others;

how he rescued Sita from Ravana's captivity in Lanka with the help of an army of monkeys and bears; how he returned to Ayodhya and was crowned as the king; how he banished Sita to the forest after a false accusation by a washerman; how he ruled his kingdom with justice and righteousness; and how he finally left the world and returned to his original form of Vishnu.

Narada told Valmiki that Rama's story was not only a historical account, but also a sacred scripture. He told him that Rama's story was the essence of Hindu dharma, the eternal law of righteousness.

He then asked Valmiki to write down Rama's story in a poetic form for the benefit of mankind. He told him that he was the chosen one to do this task, as he had been blessed by Rama himself.

Valmiki agreed to do so. He felt inspired and honoured by Narada's request.

He then composed the Ramayana, the epic poem that narrated Rama's story in 24,000 verses and seven chapters. He used the shloka metre, which consisted of two lines of sixteen syllables each. He also used various literary devices, such as similes, metaphors, alliterations, rhymes, puns, and others.

He wrote the Ramayana with great skill and devotion. He wrote it not only as a poet, but also as a sage and a teacher.

He wrote it not only as a story, but also as a philosophy and a religion.

He wrote it not only for his own satisfaction, but also for the welfare of the world.

He wrote it not only for his own time, but also for all times.

He wrote it not only for India, but also for the world.

He wrote it not only for Hindus, but also for all humanity.

Valmiki then taught the Ramayana to his disciples, who spread it across India and beyond. He also taught it to Lava and Kusha, who were Rama's sons born to Sita in his hermitage. He raised them as his own sons and taught them everything about their father and mother.

He also gave them a chance to meet their father when he came to perform a horse sacrifice near his hermitage. He asked them to sing the Ramayana in front of him and his court.

Lava and Kusha sang the Ramayana with great beauty and grace. They captivated everyone with their voice and talent.

They also surprised everyone with their identity and parentage.

They reunited Rama with Sita and proved her innocence and purity.

They then returned to Ayodhya with their parents and lived happily ever after.

Valmiki's story is one of the most inspiring and influential stories in Hindu mythology and Indian literature. It is a story of transformation, inspiration, legacy, poetry, sagehood, teaching, writing, Ramayana, shloka, dharma.

It is a story that teaches us many lessons about life and values.

It is a story that we should always admire.

Gandhari: A Blindfolded Queen's Power and Grace

A long time ago, in ancient India, there was a blindfolded queen named Gandhari. She was the wife of Dhritarashtra, the king of Hastinapura, and the mother of a hundred sons, the Kauravas. She was also the sister of Shakuni, the king of Gandhara, and the aunt of the Pandavas, the sons of Pandu, Dhritarashtra's younger brother. She played a prominent role in the Hindu epic the Mahabharata, which narrated the story of the war between the Kauravas and the Pandavas for the throne of Hastinapura.

Gandhari was born as a princess of Gandhara, a kingdom located in present-day Afghanistan and Pakistan. She was a devotee of Lord Shiva and had impressed him with her penance and piety. He had granted her a boon to bear a hundred sons. She was also known for her beauty and virtue.

Her marriage was arranged with Dhritarashtra, the eldest son of Vichitravirya, the king of Hastinapura. He was born blind due to a curse by his father's first wife Ambika, who had closed her eyes when she saw him for the first time. He was denied the throne because of his disability and his younger brother Pandu became the king instead.

Gandhari's marriage was arranged by Bhishma, the son of Shantanu, the previous king of Hastinapura, and Ganga, the goddess of river Ganga. He was also Dhritarashtra's uncle and guardian. He had vowed to remain celibate and serve the throne of Hastinapura for his whole life. He had chosen Gandhari as Dhritarashtra's bride because of her desire to bear a hundred sons, which would ensure the continuity of the Kuru dynasty.

When Gandhari learned that her husband-to-be was blind, she decided to blindfold herself as a sign of loyalty and love. She also wanted to share his experiences and challenges as a blind person. She vowed to never remove her blindfold until her death.

She married Dhritarashtra and became his queen. She loved him dearly and supported him in his duties and decisions. She also bore him a hundred sons and one daughter. The eldest son was Duryodhana, who became the crown prince of Hastinapura. The other sons were Dushasana, Vikarna, Chitrasena, Vivimsati, Durmukha, Dussaha, Durmada, Durdhara, Durmarshana, Durvishaha, Durjaya, Dussalan, Jalagandha, Sama, Saha, Vindha, Anuvindha, Durdharsha, Subahu, Dushpradharsha, Durvimochana, Ayobaahu , Mahabaahu , Chitrabaahu , Nishangin , Pasenadi , Ugrasrava , Ugrasena , Senani , Dushkarna , Karna , Vrishasena , Vrishaketu , Chitrasena , Satyasena ,

Sushena , Shatrunjaya , Dvipata , Shatadhanwan , Ugrayudha , Bhurivala , Jayatsena , Bhurisrava , Sala , Bhima , Vrika , Ashvatthama , Kripa , Kritavarma , Shalya , Shakuni , Duhsala (daughter) and Yuyutsu (stepson).

Gandhari was also a powerful and graceful queen. She had acquired immense spiritual power due to her devotion to Lord Shiva and her blindfolded life. She could see through her inner eye and sense things beyond normal perception. She could also bless or curse anyone with her words.

She used her power for good most of the time. She blessed many people with happiness and prosperity. She also cursed some people who deserved it.

She blessed Kunti, Pandu's first wife and the mother of three Pandavas - Yudhishthira, Bhima and Arjuna - with another son after she lost her husband due to a curse by Sage Kindama. She also blessed Madri, Pandu's second wife and the mother of two Pandavas - Nakula and Sahadeva - with another son after she followed her husband in death by self-immolation.

She cursed Duryodhana's thigh to be broken by Bhima in the final duel of the war, after he tried to insult her daughter-in-law Draupadi, the wife of the five Pandavas, by showing his thigh to her in a suggestive manner. She also cursed Shakuni's dice to be destroyed by Vidura, Dhritarashtra's half-brother and minister, after he used them to cheat the Pandavas in a game of dice and caused their exile for thirteen years.

However, she also used her power for evil sometimes. She cursed Lord Krishna, the avatar of Lord Vishnu and the guide and friend of the Pandavas, to die a lonely and painful death, after he failed to prevent the war between the Kauravas and the Pandavas, which resulted in the death of all her sons and grandsons. She also cursed the Yadava clan, Krishna's relatives and allies, to be destroyed by infighting and madness.

Gandhari was also a conflicted and tragic queen. She was torn between her love for her husband and sons and her duty towards her brother and nephews. She was also torn between her loyalty to the Kaurava side and her sympathy for the Pandava side.

She tried to be fair and just to both sides. She tried to stop the war and bring peace between them. She tried to advise and correct her husband and sons when they did wrong. She tried to console and support her brother and nephews when they suffered.

However, she also failed to prevent or stop the evil deeds of her husband and sons. She failed to stop Duryodhana from plotting against the Pandavas. She failed to stop Dushasana from dragging Draupadi by her hair into the court. She failed to stop Karna from calling Draupadi a whore. She failed to stop Shakuni from manipulating Duryodhana into gambling away his kingdom and his brothers.

She also failed to save or protect her husband and sons from their enemies. She failed to save Duryodhana from Bhima's mace. She failed to save Dushasana from Bhima's hands. She failed to save Karna from Arjuna's arrow. She failed to save Shakuni from Sahadeva's sword.

She also failed to live or die with dignity and grace. She lived a life of blindness and sorrow. She died a death of loneliness and despair.

She was a blindfolded queen who had power and grace, but also conflict and tragedy.

She was Gandhari, one of the most complex and fascinating characters in Hindu mythology and Indian literature.

I hope you enjoyed reading this collection of stories. I would like to thank you for choosing this book and for giving me the opportunity to share these stories with you. I would also like to acknowledge the original sources of these stories, which are the treasures of Hindu mythology and Indian literature. Without them, this book would not have been possible.

I invite you to explore more stories from these sources, as well as from other cultures and traditions. Stories are the bridges that connect us to our past, present, and future. Stories are the mirrors that reflect our values, beliefs, and aspirations. Stories are the windows that open up new perspectives, insights, and possibilities.

Thank you for being a part of this journey of stories. I hope you will continue to discover and enjoy more stories in your life.

These stories are based on various resources and may not contain the exact mythological stories, but may have the sufficient morals one needs to learn in order to succeed in life. Most of the information was based on research using various search engines and stuff. I request your apology if any content was depicted to affect the feelings of any person, group, or communities.

Thank you so much for reading up to here.

-   ACHINTYA